Racer Series

Jeff Gordon

John Regruth

MBI Publishing Company

First published in 2001 by MBI Publishing Company, Galtier Plaza, Suite 200, 380 Jackson Street, St. Paul, MN 55101-3885 USA

MBI Publishing Company books are also available at discounts in bulk quantity for industrial or sales-promotional use. For details write to Special Sales Manager at Motorbooks International Wholesalers & Distributors, 729 Prospect Avenue, PO Box 1, Osceola, WI 54020-0001 USA.

Library of Congress Cataloging-in-Publication Data

Regruth, John C.
   Jeff Gordon / John C. Regruth & William Burt.
      p. cm. — (Racer series)
   Includes index.
   ISBN 0-7603-0952-3 (pbk. : alk. paper)

1. Gordon, Jeff, 1971–2. Automobile racing drivers—United States—Biography. I. Burt, William M. II. Title. III. Series

GV1032.G67 R44 2001
796.72'092—dc21

On the front cover: Over the course of his Winston Cup career, Jeff Gordon has had a lot to smile about. No other driver in stock car racing history has managed to achieve what Gordon has in such a short period of time. In nine years, he has won over 55 races, 3 championships, and has scored 6 consecutive road course wins.

On the frontispiece: Jeff Gordon climbs into the familiar No. 24 DuPont Chevy at the last race of the 1999 season at Atlanta. *Dale L. Stringer*

On the title page: Mark Martin and Steve Park hound Jeff Gordon at the 2001 New England 300 at New Hampshire International Speedway. Gordon started on the pole and finished 2nd behind race-winner Dale Jarrett. Park held on to finish a respectable 6th, while Martin faded back to 18th. *Nigel Kinrade*

On the back cover: The Hendrick Motorsports team otherwise known as the "Rainbow Warriors" wheel the No. 24 back to the garage area after turning laps in preparation for the 1995 Brickyard 400. *Sean Stringer*

Designed by: Dan Perry

Printed in Hong Kong

Contents

One of the many triumphs in Jeff Gordon's 1998 championship winning season came at the Pocono's Pennsylvania 500. Jeff Gordon seized victory ahead of Mark Martin, Jeff Burton and Bobby Labonte. Here, Gordon celebrates the fine victory with his wife Brooke and other members of Hendrick Motorsports team.
Nigel Kinrade

Quick Facts about Jeff Gordon's Winston Cup Career

Number of races run before 1st victory	42
Most consecutive victories	4 (1998 7/26—Pocono, 8/1— Indianapolis, 8/9—Watkins Glen, 8/16—Michigan)
Most consecutive races without a victory (after 1st victory)	13— twice (199495 & 1999–2000)
Most consecutive Top 5 finishes	17 (1998)
Most consecutive Top 10 finishes	21 (1998–99)
Fewest points earned in a race	34 (1999 at Texas)
Number of times earned maximum points (185)	28 (1994 [1 time], 1995 [6], 1996 [6], 1997 [4], 1998 [6], 1999 [4], 2000 [1]
Most wins in a season	13—1998
Most DNFs in a season	11—1993
Fewest DNFs in a season	2—1997, 1998
Largest single-race prize	$2,172,246 (1999 Daytona 500)
Smallest single-race prize	$4,180 (1993 First Union 400/North Wilkesboro)
Number of provisionals taken, career	0
Number of poles	32
Worst starting position	40 (1994 Winston 500/Talladega)
Worst finish	43 (1999 Primestar 500/Texas)
Earliest point in calendar year to win	February 16 (1997 Daytona 500)
Lowest position in point standings	43 (1996—Week 2)
Lowest finish in point standings	14 (1993)
Number of times led the most laps	42 (1994 [1 time], 1995 [11], 1996 [10], 1997 [4], 1998 [8], 1999 [6], 2000 [2]
Most laps led in a single race	431 of 500 (1997 Goody's Headache Powder 500/Martinsville)
Highest percentage of laps led, race	93.8—375 of 400 (1998 MBNA Platinum 400/Dover)
Most laps led in a season	2,600 (1995)
Highest percentage of laps led, season	26.4 (1995)
Least number of laps completed in a race	13 of 200 (1996 Daytona 500)
Tracks where Gordon has won	Atlanta, Bristol, California, Charlotte, Darlington, Daytona, Dover, Indianapolis, Martinsville, Michigan, New Hampshire, North Wilkesboro, Pocono, Richmond, Rockingham, Sears Point, Talladega, Watkins Glen
Tracks where Gordon has not won	Homestead, Las Vegas, Phoenix, Texas
Tracks where Gordon has won a pole	Atlanta, California, Charlotte, Darlington, Daytona, Dover, Indianapolis, Martinsville, Michigan, New Hampshire, North Wilkesboro, Pocono, Richmond, Rockingham, Sears Point, Watkins Glen
Tracks where Gordon has not won a pole	Bristol, Homestead, Las Vegas, Phoenix, Talladega, Texas
Track where Gordon has won the most poles	Charlotte (7)
Track where Gordon has the most wins	Darlington (5)
Most lucrative track, career	Daytona ($3,811,927)
Worst-to-First: Worst starting spot in an eventual victory	36th (2000 DieHard 500/Talladega)
First-to-Worst: Worst finish after starting from the pole	39th (2000 UAW-GM Quality 500/Charlotte)
Favorite starting spot in victories	1st (11 victories)
No. of times won from the pole	11

Gordon's Place

The excitement surrounding Jeff Gordon during his magical run in the 1990s reached its giddiest heights in 1998 when a racing reporter projected the year the young driver would catch and surpass Richard Petty's all-time NASCAR record of 200 victories. At this pace, the story went, a 46-year-old Gordon would match the King's record in the year 2016. The projection assumed about nine wins per season, a pace Gordon actually exceeded between 1995 and 1998. Though clearly ridiculous—Petty's untouchable record is best compared to major league baseball's unbreakable mark, pitcher Cy Young's 511 wins—the thought behind that projection is interesting. Where, exactly, does Gordon fit in NASCAR history?

A more immediate way to ask the same question is, "If Jeff Gordon retired today, where would he stack up?" The short, hypothetical answer: Supposing early retirement, Gordon's career would best be described as a cross between the careers of Fred Lorenzen and Darrell Waltrip. Lorenzen because he would have retired too soon after displaying an uncommon ability to win races early and often. Waltrip because he has proven himself through Winston Cup titles, wins, and poles to be one of the greatest drivers in NASCAR history, and one of the most unpopular because of that

One of the most memorable moments in a career filled with them. Here Gordon triumphantly raises the winner's trophy following his stirring victory in the inaugural 1994 Brickyard 400 at Indianapolis. With the victory, the then-23-year-old driver forever linked his name with Ray Harroun, winner of the first-ever Indianapolis 500 in 1911 and, later, Michael Schumacher, who won the inaugural U.S. Grand Prix Formula 1 event in September 2000.

From 1995 through 1999, Jeff Gordon was NASCAR's best driver. In that time, he led the Winston Cup series in wins, money, Top 5s, laps led, poles, races led, average start, and average finish. His three championships established him as one of the greatest drivers in NASCAR history.

must be considered one of the true legends in stock car racing history. But with a single championship (in 1983), he does not command as much historical clout as Darrell Waltrip (84 wins, 3 championships), Cale Yarborough (83 wins, 3 championships), or even Terry Labonte (21 wins, 2 championships).

Winning races, of course, still counts for a lot. Victories continue to differentiate great drivers from good ones. Great drivers who lack a championship have lifted themselves from the pack in NASCAR history through frequent trips to Victory Lane. Winning drivers such as Lorenzen, Junior Johnson, Mark Martin, Ricky Rudd, Davey Allison, and Geoffrey Bodine enjoy a heightened level of historic respect despite being title-starved. A step above this group in NASCAR's hierarchy are the championship winners. Distinguished by their ability to sustain excellence over the course of a full season, drivers such as Alan Kulwicki, Bobby Allison,

success.

The long answer to the question of Gordon's place is more complex. After more than half a century of NASCAR racing, a hierarchy of greatness has emerged. Particularly since NASCAR shortened and sharpened the focus of its schedule and ushered in the modern era in 1972, the Winston Cup championship has come to define greatness. Victories, poles, Top 5s, and prize winnings are powerful cards in the deck, but winning the championship trumps all. To illustrate, Bobby Allison—85 wins, 59 poles, 446 Top 10s—

Since NASCAR ushered in the modern era in 1972, the Winston Cup championship has come to define greatness. Gordon and two other Winston Cup champions battle for position during the 1998 DieHard 500 on the high banks of Talladega. Seven-time champion Dale Earnhardt trails three-time champ Gordon. Recently crowned 2000 champion Bobby Labonte uses the low line to make a move.

NASCAR fans love to hate a winner and Gordon's extreme success has created extreme animosity. The loudest reaction heard at Winston Cup tracks these days is the booing and jeering hurled at Gordon when his name is spoken over the public address system. Pre-race driver introductions have become anti-Gordon rallies. Here, Gordon politely waves to a booing crowd during driver intros at Rockingham.

Gordon currently sits at the second highest level of NASCAR greatness, with perhaps another two decades of competition ahead of him. Only seven-time winners Dale Earnhardt and Richard Petty can claim a higher degree of achievement.

Gordon supported his championship binge with the type of raw statistical excellence not seen since Yarborough's eye-popping performance during the late 1970s. Gordon's 47 wins from 1995 to 1999 are the greatest number of victories in any five-year stretch during the modern era (Darrell Waltrip's 42 wins from 1980 to 1984 is second best). From nowhere, he has risen to ninth on NASCAR's all-time career victories list. No driver has ever come closer to winning four straight championships than Gordon, who won titles in 1995, 1997, and 1998, and fell short in 1996 by a mere 37 points (to teammate Terry Labonte). In 1998, he produced a season for

Rusty Wallace, Dale Jarrett, and Bobby Labonte earned an elevated spot in NASCAR history by winning the Winston Cup. Two-time championship winners, Terry Labonte, Ned Jarrett, and Buck Baker among them, have risen even higher in historic perspective.

At the pinnacle of NASCAR greatness are the drivers who have won three or more championships. Gordon reached these heights after winning three championships in four years between 1995 and 1998. Only six other drivers have risen as high as Gordon in NASCAR history. Unlike the others, he did it before his 28th birthday. Joining legends Waltrip, Yarborough, David Pearson, and Lee Petty,

The re-introduction of the Monte Carlo in 1995 propelled Gordon to new heights. As the lead development team for the 1995 Monte Carlo, Gordon enjoyed a head start on the competition when the new car took the Winston Cup series by storm. While driving the car in five seasons, Gordon won 47 times and jumped to ninth on the all-time NASCAR victory list.

the ages, winning a modern-era record-tying 13 races, earning an all-time record $9.3 million, piling up the greatest number of points ever under the current point system (5,328), and becoming the first driver to reach 5,000 points since Yarborough in 1977. Between 1995 and 1999, Gordon collected more victories, poles, Top 5s, money, laps led, front row starts, and lead-lap finishes than any other driver. He also had the best average start and finish in the Winston Cup series in that time. By any measure—championships, wins, poles, money, you name it—Gordon must be considered one of the greatest NASCAR drivers ever, even if he retired today.

Interpreting Greatness

In the intensely loyal world of NASCAR, however, no claim to greatness ever goes unchallenged. Excellence is viewed suspiciously. Sustained excellence is proof of an unfair advantage. Unfortunately for all of the three-time champions in NASCAR history, circumstances have fueled these suspicions. Each of the three-time champs won their titles inside of a six-year period. Lee Petty won three times between 1954 and 1959. Waltrip's three championships came in a five-year span from 1981 to 1985. Gordon (1995–98) and Pearson (1966–69) won three times in four years. Yarborough, meanwhile, is the only driver to win three straight championships. While each driver's achievement is remarkable, the short span within which each was accomplished suggests a perfect owner-driver-team-car combination was found. Or perhaps some advantage was discovered that propelled the driver and his team to impressive heights before the rest of the field closed the gap. Most suspiciously, perhaps NASCAR officials allowed an unfair advantage, consciously or unconsciously, to go unchecked.

Yarborough and especially Waltrip

The Jeff Gordon–Ray Evernham combination proved to be one of the greatest in NASCAR history. Evernham became Gordon's crew chief when the young driver joined the Busch Grand National series in 1991. They stayed together when Gordon made the leap to the Winston Cup series in 1993. In their 278 Busch and Winston Cup starts, they won 50 races and 42 poles. Their success sparked heated debate: Was Gordon's success a result of talent or Evernham's mechanical brilliance?

Resentment to Gordon's success reached its peak in 1998 when Jack Roush—car owner for Mark Martin—accused the Hendrick team of cheating by using an illegal tire-softening agent. NASCAR investigations found no evidence of the substance. Gordon responded by beating second-place Martin in the final point standings by 364 points. Here, Gordon and Martin line up side-by-side for the 1996 Brickyard 400.

grandstands, manifested itself most explosively in late 1998 when Jack Roush, a partisan Ford owner, accused Gordon of cheating following his victory at New Hampshire. Roush charged that Gordon's team used an illegal softening agent on its tires, which allowed better grip on the track and, therefore, faster lap times. In reaction to Roush's accusation, NASCAR pounced. The sanctioning body confiscated Gordon's car and all of the tires distributed to the team that weekend. Extensive testing of the tires was conducted but revealed no evidence supporting Roush's contention. Illustrating

With the loss of his crew chief, crew, and car in 1999, Gordon, in a sense, became a rookie again in 2000. Of course, Gordon has never been an ordinary rookie, revealing an ability to learn and master circumstances quickly. He showed his quick-learner characteristics in the Busch series in 1991 and 1992. In 1999, Gordon returned to the Busch series in a sponsorship deal with Pepsi. Here, Gordon races Dale Earnhardt Jr. during the NAPA 200 at Michigan in 1999.

Beginning in 1995, Victory Lane press conferences featuring Jeff Gordon became the norm. Here, Gordon entertains the media following his win in the 1997 Busch Clash at Daytona. *Nigel Kinrade*

suffered through such suspicions due to the money and muscle of Junior Johnson. Johnson was an integral factor in getting tobacco giant R. J. Reynolds' to give sponsorship dollars to NASCAR. In return for Johnson's profitable assistance, according to the anti-Johnson/Yarborough/Waltrip forces, NASCAR allowed the famous car owner greater freedom to interpret, and manipulate, the rules. The result was six Winston Cup titles for Yarborough and Waltrip in 10 seasons between 1976 and 1985.

The great Pearson also faced similar suspicions and questions after two of his titles came with the Ford-backed Holman-Moody powerhouse in 1968 and 1969.

No driver, however, has seen his efforts dismissed quite like Gordon. The reasons for his 1990s success, according to the anti-Gordon

legions, ran the gamut. From the high level: NASCAR allowed Chevy to field a clearly superior Monte Carlo in 1995 without offering redress to the Fords and Pontiacs. To the smallest of details: NASCAR allowed the diminutive Gordon to run a lighter car than, say, Jimmy Spencer, thus creating a natural advantage. The intense loyalty of NASCAR fans prevented them from allowing Gordon to enjoy unquestioned success. Some explanation had to be available for all of those victories and championships, and talent surely wasn't it. Most often stated was the belief that Gordon was simply the dumb-luck beneficiary of crew chief Ray Evernham's mastery and the bottomless resources of car owner Rick Hendrick.

Anti-Gordon sentiment, roiling since late 1996 in the form of thunderous boos from the

Before embarking on his successful stock-car racing career, Gordon built his skills and a considerable reputation on the open-wheel circuits. Here, he attacks the high banks of Salem (Indiana) Speedway in a USAC sprint car in 1988.

just how conspiratorial the NASCAR world had become of Gordon's success, Roush made a remarkable claim: The softening agent used was so subtle it could not be detected even by the most sophisticated investigative techniques. In other words, Gordon was cheating, whether Roush and NASCAR could prove it or not. In the face of such reckless charges, Gordon and his team conducted themselves with class. And they won the 1998 title by 364 points over Mark Martin, a Roush-sponsored driver.

Facing Change

Adding fuel to the anti-Gordon fires was his tumultuous 1999 season and the sometimes-regressive 2000 campaign. For the first time in his career, change was thrust upon Gordon. A record five consecutive seasons as the Winston Cup series' most prolific winner gave way to an also-ran year in 2000 in which Gordon had no impact on the point standings or on any statistical category. In 1999 he fell to sixth place in the point standings, some 642 points behind leader Dale Jarrett. In 2000, he dropped to ninth place, a staggering 769 points short of Bobby Labonte.

The main cause of Gordon's fall was a seemingly ceaseless series of significant changes: first, he lost his crew chief, then he lost his crew, then he lost his car. Evernham, Gordon's crew chief since he joined the Busch series in 1991, left to lead Dodge's re-entry into the Winston Cup series. The rainbow warriors, the over-the-wall race-day crew that redefined the concept of a pit stop, later defected to Jarrett's camp. Less often cited, but perhaps most significant to Gordon's troubles, was the release of the 2000 Monte Carlo. Back in 1995, Hendrick Motorsports was the lead development team for the Monte Carlo's re-introduction. With unrivaled knowledge about the car, Gordon's team enjoyed a tremendous head start on other Chevy teams when the 1995 season began. After winning 21 of 31 races in 1995 plus the Busch Clash, both Twin 125s, and the Winston all-star race, the Monte Carlo turned out to be a dominant car. Gordon and his Hendrick teammates were the natural beneficiaries. The advantage showed in Gordon's breakthrough results. After two wins in 1994—the first of his career—Gordon scored seven wins in 1995 and outlasted Dale Earnhardt for the championship. He followed with 10-win seasons in 1996 and 1997, then 13 in 1998.

Not interested in watching Chevy's dominance, Ford and Pontiac countered the emergence of the Monte Carlo with upgrades

One explanation offered for Gordon's ability to adapt quickly to Busch and Winston Cup stock cars is his experience driving sprint cars. Learning how to handle multiple types of sprint cars on slippery dirt tracks forced Gordon to gain instant recognition of a car's characteristics. Here, he races on dirt in a winged sprint in 1988.

of their own. Ford scrapped the aging Thunderbird and introduced the productive Taurus in 1997. Pontiac steadily improved its Grand Prix into a weekly contender. When GM looked to produce an updated version of its Monte Carlo, Hendrick Motorsports played a much less prominent role in the new car's development. The Earnhardt-Childress conglomerate took the lead research and development role and the results, as in 1995, were predictable. Earnhardt contended for an eighth championship for much of the 2000

season, while Dale Earnhardt Inc. drivers Dale Earnhardt Jr. and Steve Park excelled.

Lacking the knowledge advantage they had in 1995, Gordon and Hendrick Motorsports were forced to junk five years worth of setups and experience and learn the new car the old-fashioned way: on the track in race competition. As he entered the 2000 season, Gordon looked out on a changed world. He had to face his Winston Cup competitors with a new car, a new crew chief, and a new crew.

In a sense, Jeff Gordon became a rookie again in 2000.

A Second Rookie Season

For rival fans hoping that Gordon's success was merely the result of a warm body sitting in Ray Evernham's expertly prepared cars, the 2000 season signaled otherwise. If circumstances forced Gordon into a second rookie season, his stock-car career has demonstrated an ability to learn quickly in such situations. The pattern of Gordon's career

Above: In 1991, Gordon pulled double duty, running USAC cars and making his rookie debut in the Busch Grand National series. Pictured here in 1991 in his USAC Midget sprint car at an indoor show held at the RCA Dome in Indianapolis.

Right: Jeff Gordon takes time to sign autographs for fans at Indianapolis in August 1993. A Winston Cup rookie at the time, Gordon was at the Indianapolis Motor Speedway to take part in a two-day tire test at the hallowed track in preparation for the following summer's inaugural Brickyard 400. Though a NASCAR newcomer in 1993, Gordon, a former resident of nearby Pittsboro, was already well known in Indianapolis.

became clear in the early 1990s when he toured the Busch Grand National circuit, then jumped to the Winston Cup series in 1993. Simply put, he's a quick study. Early struggles inevitably yield to sustained excellence.

In his rookie Busch season in 1991, driving for Bill Davis Racing, Gordon looked every bit like a struggling open-wheel racer trying unsuccessfully to learn how to drive a heavy stock car. He finished the year with no wins, one pole and five Top 5 finishes. A year later, Gordon won three times, claimed an astonishing 11 poles, doubled his Top 5 finishes, and leapt to fourth in the final point

Thanks to his frequent trips to victory lane and their close relationship, Jeff and Brooke Gordon have become fixtures on the Winston Cup scene. A former Miss Winston, Brooke first met her future husband in Victory Lane in 1993 after he won a Twin 125 qualifying race at Daytona.

standings. When he moved up to Rick Hendrick's Winston Cup organization the following season at the age of 21, a similarly accelerated pattern emerged. His first two seasons produced 21 DNFs (Did Not Finish)—eight of them due to crashes—two wins and two poles. In the point standings, he climbed from 14th in his first season to eighth in his second full season. In just his third season, the struggles turned to excellence. Gordon won the 1995 Winston Cup championship, becoming the second-youngest driver ever to win a title at NASCAR's highest level (behind only 1950 champ Bill Rexford). More impressively, only Earnhardt, who won the title in his second season in 1980, won a Winston Cup championship earlier in his career.

With Gordon entering a quasi-rookie season in 2000, the pattern evident earlier in his career played out again. With nearly every tie to his past success severed (his car owner, team manager, and paint scheme among the few holdovers), he started over, learning a new car with his new crew chief Robbie Loomis and getting a feel for his new pit crew during race competition. Early efforts were marked by struggle: In 21 races in late 1999 and early 2000, he finished in the Top 5 just three times. Uncharacteristically poor qualifying (12.5 average starting position) led to uninspired finishes on race day (his average finish: 14th). For the entire 2000 season, Gordon's average start and average finish were both outside of the Top 10—the first time that happened since his rookie year in 1993.

Out of the 2000 championship race by the summer, Gordon turned his focus to learning. He involved himself in the mechanical detail of race setups. Perhaps the most startling sight was Gordon seeking setup and driving guidance from new teammate Jerry Nadeau. Though chronologically a year older than Gordon, Nadeau has less than half

Jeff Gordon in The Winston Cup Series (1995–1999)			
Money Won	$29,316,703	1st	D. Jarrett—24,047,870
Avg. Start	7.0	1st	Mark Martin—9.1
Avg. Finish	9.5	1st	Mark Martin—9.8
Wins	47	1st	Dale Jarrett—19
Top 5s	104	1st	Dale Jarrett—89
Top 10s	119	2nd	Mark Martin—121
Poles	29	1st	Bobby Labonte—17
Front Row Starts	53	1st	Bobby Labonte—28
Laps Led	9,597	1st	Dale Jarrett—5,026
Races Led	130	1st	Mark Martin—98
Times Led	416	1st	Mark Martin—263
Times Led Most Laps	39	1st	Mark Martin—20
Wins from Pole	10	1st	Martin, B. Labonte—4
Lead Lap Finishes	120	1st	Mark Martin—116

Gordon discusses car setup with his crew following a practice run. Since the departure of his longtime crew chief Ray Evernham, Gordon has taken a more active role on the mechanical side in his team's racing effort. If he can win another championship, he will separate himself from the other three-time champs and will be exonerated of any past and future suspicions about his talent.

as much "seat time" in a Winston Cup car as Gordon (not to mention 3 fewer championships and 51 fewer career victories). Putting learning ahead of pride, Gordon even took lessons from Nadeau on his best tracks, most notably Charlotte (where Gordon has won four races and seven poles) and Atlanta.

Much like his Busch and early Winston Cup experiences, the hard work resulted in accelerated success. After a frustrating first half in 2000, Gordon's team evolved rapidly and began to unload the fastest Chevy in the field each weekend. Starting with the June Pocono race, consistently strong finishes rolled in. Over the season's final 20 races, he had 15 Top 10 finishes, including 9 Top 5s. In the season's final month, covering the last five races, no driver scored more championship points than Gordon.

By the end of the 2000 season, the pattern seemed to be holding in the post-Evernham, post-Rainbow Warriors era: Early struggles gave way to sustained excellence.

New Challenge

Safely established as one of NASCAR's all-time best, Gordon has embarked on the next great challenge of his career: joining Earnhardt and Petty as the only drivers to claim a fourth title. Like the two greatest drivers in NASCAR history, Gordon will have to prove his talent is deep enough to span years and changes in crew chiefs, team personnel, and car models. Petty and Earnhardt separated themselves from NASCAR's three-time champions by winning titles over extended periods of time. Petty won his seven championships in 16 years between 1964 and 1979. Earnhardt collected seven titles

over 15 years from 1980 to 1994, including three sets of back-to-back championships. Earnhardt won championships in different cars (Monte Carlo and Lumina) with different car owners (Rod Osterlund and Richard Childress) and with different crew chiefs. Thanks to recent changes within his team, Gordon has a similar opportunity to demonstrate his ability to win regardless of personnel or machinery.

The 2001 and 2002 seasons will define a new stage in Gordon's career. If he can win another championship, he will separate himself from the other three-time champs and will be exonerated of any past and future suspicions about his talent. Still less than 30 years old, with perhaps less than a third of his career complete, Gordon is poised to move beyond the three-time-title gang and secure an even higher place in NASCAR history.

Chapter 1

A Statistical Breakdown of Jeff Gordon's Career Performance

The following section offers the bottom-line statistical view of Jeff Gordon's career. Year-by-year and career totals are listed, including wins, Top 5s, Top 10s, poles, average start and finish, DNFs, total championship and bonus points, points per race, total winnings, races led, percentage of laps led, and lead-lap finishes.

· Career Start-Finish Breakdown—A complete breakdown of Gordon's starts and finishes throughout his career
· Career Poles—A complete listing of Gordon's pole starts
· Career Wins—A complete listing of Gordon's victories
· Career Performance by Track—Gordon's career totals at each track, broken out by track type

Hendrick Motorsports crewmen work on the No. 24 Chevy Monte Carlo at Talladega. Like all drivers, Gordon relies on his behind-the-scenes and under-the-hood team to provide winning cars. The money and manpower of the multi-car Hendrick Motorsports helped lure Gordon away from his Busch Series car owner, Bill Davis, in 1993 and, in 2000, convinced Gordon to sign a lifetime contract with the Hendrick organization.

Year	Final Standing	Races Run	Wins	Top 5s	Top 10s	Poles	Avg Start	Avg. Finish	DNFs	Total Points	Bonus Points	Points Per Race	Total Winnings	Races Led	Laps Led	Pct. Led	On Lead Lap	Pct. on Lead Lap
1992	—	1	0	0	0	0	21.0	31.0	1	70	0	70.0	$6,285	0	0	0.0	0	0.00
1993	14th	30	0	7	11	1	13.1	17.7	11	3,447	70	114.9	765,168	14	230	2.3	11	36.7
1994	8th	31	2	7	14	1	9.8	15.8	10	3,776	90	121.8	1,779,523	17	446	4.4	10	32.3
1995	1st	31	7	17	23	8	5.0	9.5	3	4,614	200	148.8	4,347,343	29	2,600	26.4	23	74.2
1996	2nd	31	10	21	24	5	6.3	9.5	5	4,620	175	149.0	3,428,485	25	2,314	24.0	24	77.4
1997	1st	32	10	22	23	1	9.4	9.6	2	4,710	140	147.2	6,375,658	24	1,647	16.8	22	68.8
1998	1st	33	13	26	28	7	6.9	5.7	2	5,328	170	161.5	9,306,584	26	1,717	17.3	28	84.9
1999	6th	34	7	18	21	7	7.4	12.9	7	4,620	160	135.9	5,858,633	26	1,319	13.0	23	67.7
2000	9th	34	3	11	22	3	12.2	12.9	3	4,361	85	128.3	2,703,586	15	425	4.2	22	64.7
Totals		**257**	**52**	**129**	**166**	**33**	**8.8**	**11.7**	**44**	**35,546**	**1,090**	**138.3**	**$34,571,265**	**176**	**10,698**	**13.4**	**163**	**63.4**

The distinctive rainbow-colored paint scheme worn by Gordon's No. 24 Chevy from 1992 to 2000 made it one of the most recognizable cars in the Winston Cup series.

a

Career Start Breakdown

Pos.	No. of Starts	Pct.
Pole*	34	13.2
2	26	10.1
3	26	10.1
4	16	6.2
5	19	7.4
6	12	4.7
7	12	4.7
8	14	5.4
9	7	2.7
10	7	2.7
11	11	4.3
12	9	3.5
13	7	2.7
14	5	1.9
15	7	2.7
16	4	1.6
17	5	1.9
18	1	0.4
19	3	1.2
20	1	0.4
21	8	3.1
22	2	0.8
23	4	1.6
24	3	1.2
25	1	0.4
26	2	0.8
27	1	0.4
28	2	0.8
29	3	1.2
30	1	0.4
31	0	—
32	0	—
33	0	—
34	1	0.4
35	0	—
36	1	0.4
37	1	0.4
38	0	—
39	0	—
40	1	0.4
41	0	—
42	0	—
43	0	—

Career Start Statistics

Average Start	8.81
Front Row Starts (Pct.)	60 (23.3)
Top 5	121 (47.1)
Top 10	173 (67.3)
Top 20	226 (87.9)
Top 30	253 (98.4)
Pos. 31—43	4 (1.6)
Provisionals	0

Career Finish Breakdown

Pos.	No. of Finishes	Pct.
Win	52	20.2
2	24	9.3
3	22	8.6
4	15	5.8
5	16	6.2
6	11	4.3
7	7	2.7
8	10	3.9
9	3	1.2
10	6	2.3
11	7	2.7
12	3	1.2
13	1	0.4
14	2	0.8
15	3	1.2
16	2	0.8
17	5	1.9
18	1	0.4
19	1	0.4
20	2	0.8
21	3	1.2
22	3	1.2
23	3	1.2
24	3	1.2
25	1	0.4
26	1	0.4
27	0	—
28	3	1.2
29	1	0.4
30	2	0.8
31	9	3.5
32	6	2.3
33	4	1.6
34	5	1.9
35	3	1.2
36	2	0.8
37	4	1.6
38	2	0.8
39	4	1.6
40	2	0.8
41	0	—
42	2	0.8
43	1	0.4

Career Finish Statistics

Total Races	257
Average Finish	11.72
Top 2 (Pct.)	76 (29.6)
Top 5	129 (50.2)
Top 10	166 (64.6)
Top 20	193 (75.1)
Top 30	213 (82.9)
Pos. 31 – 43	44 (17.1)

* — Indicates number of starts from pole position, not number of poles won.
See Listing of Pole Starts for more detail.

Year	Career Race	No.	Track/Race	Speed	Fin.
1993	28	1	Charlotte — Mello Yello 500	177.684	5
1994	42	2	Charlotte — Coca-Cola 600	181.439	1
1995	64	3	Rockingham — Goodwrench 500	157.620	1
	65	4	Richmond — Pontiac Excitement 400	124.757	36
	67	5	Darlington — TranSouth Financial 400	170.833	32
	69	6	North Wilkesboro — First Union 400	118.765	2
	73	7	Charlotte — Coca-Cola 600	183.861	33
	74	8	Dover — Miller Genuine Draft 500	153.669	6
	76	9	Michigan — Miller Genuine Draft 400	186.611	2
	81	10	Indianapolis — Brickyard 400	172.536	6
	88	*	Martinsville — Goody's 500	Field set by points	7
1996	104	11	Charlotte — Coca-Cola 600	183.773	4
	105	12	Dover — Miller 500	154.785	1
	106	13	Pocono — UAW-GM Teamwork 500	169.725	1
	108	14	Daytona — Pepsi 400	188.869	3
	112	15	Indianapolis — Brickyard 400	176.419	37
1997	135	16	Charlotte — Coca-Cola 600	184.300	1
1998	166	17	California — California 500	181.772	4
	167	18	Charlotte — Coca-Cola 600	182.976	1
	169	19	Richmond — Pontiac Excitement 400	125.558	37
	171	20	Pocono — Pocono 500	168.042	2
	172	21	Sears Point — Save Mart/Kragen 350	98.711	1
	176	22	Watkins Glen — The Bud at the Glen	120.331	1
	179	23	New Hampshire —— Farm Aid on CMT 300	129.033	1
1999	190	24	Daytona —— Daytona 500	195.067	1
	194	25	Darlington —— TranSouth Financial 400	173.167	3
	200	26	Richmond —— Pontiac Excitement 400[1]	126.499	31
	203	27	Michigan —— Kmart 400	186.945	2
	205	28	Sears Point — Save Mart/Kragen 350k	98.519	1
	207	29	New Hampshire — Jiffy Lube 300	131.171	3
	209	30	Indianapolis — Brickyard 400	179.612	3
2000	228	31	Darlington — Mall.com 400	172.662	8
	252	32	Charlotte — UAW-GM Quality 500	185.561	39
	257	33	Atlanta — NAPA 500	194.274	4

[1] — Track Record

Pole Statistics

No. of Poles	33
Avg. Finished after Pole Starts	9.41
Wins from the Pole	11
No. of Track Records	1
Fastest Pole Speed	195.067
Slowest Pole Speed	98.519

Gordon celebrates his win in the inaugural Brickyard 400 with an emotional victory lap around the 2.5-mile Indianapolis Motor Speedway. Gordon used the celebratory lap to salute the huge crowd, estimated to be 300,000 strong, which had adopted him as a "hometown boy."

Crewmembers set up the Dupont pit stall at North Wilkesboro during the early hours of race day in 1995. Gordon's pit crew revolutionized the role that the over-the-wall team can play in a team's success. Consisting of athletes rather than shop mechanics, Gordon's pit crew became famous for getting the No. 24 Chevy out of the pits quickly.

Every season from 1995 through 2000, Jeff Gordon competed in the International Race of Champions (IROC) series against top IRL, CART, Winston Cup, and Busch Grand National drivers. In the first-ever IROC race at Indianapolis in 1998, Gordon got caught in an early wreck involving Arie Luyendyk and finished ninth.

Year	Career Race	No.	Track—Race	Start Pos.	Laps/Led	Pct. Led	Money
1994	42	1	Charlotte—Coca-Cola 600	1	400/16	4.0	$196,500
	50	2	* Indianapolis—Brickyard 400	2	160/93	58.1	613,000
1995	64	3	Rockingham—Goodwrench Service 500	1	492/329	66.9	167,600
	66	4	Atlanta—Purolator 500	3	328/250	76.2	104,950
	68	5	Bristol—Food City 500	2	500/205	41.0	67,645
	77	6	Daytona—Pepsi 400	3	160/72	45.0	96,580
	78	7	New Hampshire—Slick 50 300	21	300/126	42.0	160,300
	85	8	Darlington—Mountain Dew Southern 500	5	367/54	14.7	70,630
	87	9	Dover—MBNA 500	2	500/400	80.0	74,655
1996	96	10	Richmond—Pontiac Excitement 400	2	400/124	31.0	92,400
	98	11	Darlington—TranSouth Financial 400	2	293/189	64.5	97,310
	99	12	Bristol—Food City 500	8	342/148	43.3	93,765
	105	13	Dover—Miller 500	1	500/307	61.4	138,730
	106	14	Pocono—UAW/GM Teamwork 500	1	200/94	47.0	96,980
	111	15	Talladega—DieHard 500	2	129/37	28.7	272,550
	116	16	Darlington—Mountain Dew Southern 500	2	367/52	14.2	99,630
	118	17	Dover—MBNA 500	3	500/203	40.6	153,630
	119	18	Martinsville—Hanes 500	10	500/133	26.6	93,825
	120	19	^ North Wilkesboro—Tyson/Holly Farms 400	2	400/207	51.8	91,350
1997	125	20	Daytona—Daytona 500	6	200/40	20.0	377,410
	126	21	Rockingham—Goodwrench Service 400	4	393/43	10.9	93,115
	131	22	Bristol—Food City 500	5	500/125	25.0	83,640
	132	23	Martinsville—Goody's Headache Powder 500	4	500/431	86.2	99,225
	135	24	Charlotte—Coca-Cola 600	1	333/44	13.2	224,900
	137	25	Pocono—Pocono 500	11	200/59	29.5	166,080
	139	26	* California—California 500	3	250/113	45.2	144,600
	144	27	Watkins Glen—Bud at the Glen	11	90/32	35.6	139,120
	147	28	# Darlington—Mountain Dew Southern 500	7	367/116	31.6	1,131,330
	149	29	New Hampshire—CMT 300	13	300/107	35.7	188,625
1998	158	30	Rockingham—GM Goodwrench Service 400	4	393/73	18.6	90,090
	162	31	Bristol—Food City 500	2	500/63	12.6	90,860
	167	32	Charlotte—Coca-Cola 600	1	400/53	13.3	429,950
	172	33	Sears Point—Save Mart/Kragen 350	1	112/47	42.0	160,675
	174	34	Pocono—Pennsylvania 500	2	200/164	82.0	165,495
	175	35	$ Indianapolis—Brickyard 400	3	160/97	60.6	1,637,625
	176	36	Watkins Glen—Bud at the Glen	1	90/57	63.3	152,970
	177	37	Michigan—Pepsi 400	3	200/8	4.0	120,302
	179	38	New Hampshire—Farm Aid on CMT 300	1	300/67	22.3	205,400
	180	39	$ Darlington—Pepsi Southern 500	5	367/64	17.4	1,134,655
	186	40	Daytona—Pepsi 400	8	160/49	30.6	184,325
	188	41	Rockingham—AC Delco 400	9	393/28	7.1	111,575
	189	42	Atlanta—NAPA 500	21	221/113	51.1	164,450
1999	190	43	$ Daytona—Daytona 500	1	200/17	8.5	2,172,246

	193	44	Atlanta—Cracker Barrel 500	8	325/109	33.5	117,650
	199	45	California—California 500	5	250/151	60.4	155,890
	205	46	Sears Point—SaveMart Supermarkets 300	1	112/80	71.4	125,040
	210	47	Watkins Glen—Frontier at the Glen	3	90/55	61.1	119,860
	217	48	Martinsville—NAPA AutoCare 500	5	500/29	5.8	110,090
	218	49	Charlotte—UAW-GM Quality 500	22	334/16	4.8	140,350
2000	232	50	Talladega—DieHard 500	36	188/25	13.3	159,755
	239	51	Sears Point—Save Mart/Kragen 300	5	112/43	38.4	143,025
	248	52	Richmond—Chevy Monte Carlo 400	13	400/15	3.8	130,220

$ — denotes won No Bull Million bonus
# — denotes won Winston Million bonus
* — denotes inaugural race
^ — denotes final race at track

Victory Statistics

No. of Victories	52
Avg. Starting Position	5.73
Favorite Starting Spot in Victories	1 (11 times)
Total Victory Earnings	$13,452,573
Laps Led (Pct.)	5,572 (34.87)
Fewest Laps Led in a Win	8
Most Laps Led in a Win	431
Highest Pct. Led	86.2
Lowest Pct. Led	3.8

"I think Jeff Gordon is the best driver who's ever driven a stock car. If his team had been using Fords this year, he might be undefeated."
—Felix Sabates, Winston Cup car owner, on Gordon's 1998 performance, *Sport Magazine*

Jeff Gordon's Career Performance on Current and Former Winston Cup Tracks

Track	Track Length	No. of Races	Wins	Win Pct.	Top 5s	Top 10s	Poles	Avg. Start	Avg. Finish	DNFs	Total Winnings	Races Led	Laps Led	Pct. Led	Total Points	Points/ Race
Short Tracks																
Bristol	.533	16	4	25.0	7	10	0	5.5	11.5	4	783,165	11	1,281	16.3	2,228	139.3
Martinsville	.526	16	3	18.8	10	13	0	8.4	6.6	0	834,955	10	1,034	13.2	2,479	154.9
North Wilkesboro	.626	8	1	12.5	4	5	1	10.1	12.4	2	278,600	3	314	9.8	1,082	135.3
Richmond	.750	16	2	12.5	8	11	3	6.9	12.4	3	833,005	12	546	8.5	2,090	130.6
Totals		**56**	**10**	**17.9**	**29**	**39**	**4**	**7.4**	**10.5**	**9**	**$2,729,725**	**36**	**3,175**	**12.6**	**7,879**	**140.7**
1-mile Ovals																
Dover	1.0	16	3	18.8	7	10	2	7.9	10.3	2	1,000,300	11	1,650	22.6	2,288	143.0
New Hampshire	1.058	12	3	25.0	7	9	2	11.1	10.7	2	1,119,890	8	529	14.8	1,717	143.1
Phoenix	1.0	8	0	0.0	3	6	0	11.9	11.3	1	349,970	2	49	2.0	1,076	134.5
Rockingham	1.017	16	4	25.0	6	7	1	6.3	16.1	5	893,185	11	765	11.3	1,977	123.6
Totals		**52**	**10**	**19.2**	**23**	**32**	**5**	**8.8**	**12.3**	**10**	**$3,353,345**	**32**	**2,993**	**14.9**	**7,058**	**135.7**
Speedways (1–2 miles)																
Atlanta	1.5	17	3	17.6	7	9	1	12.9	15.2	4	947,705	10	624	11.4	2,149	126.4
Charlotte	1.5	16	4	25.0	9	10	7	7.1	14.7	4	1,731,850	15	364	6.3	2,082	130.1
Darlington	1.336	16	5	31.3	9	11	3	7.0	9.6	3	3,013,670	13	788	15.5	2,351	146.9
Homestead	1.5	2	0	0.0	0	2	0	19.0	8.5	0	154,315	1	3	0.6	285	142.5
Las Vegas	1.5	3	0	0.0	1	1	0	8.7	16.0	0	326,475	1	1	.002	361	120.3
Texas	1.5	4	0	0.0	0	0	0	12.5	32.3	2	263,250	1	69	5.2	270	67.5
Totals		**58**	**12**	**20.7**	**26**	**33**	**11**	**9.0**	**14.2**	**13**	**$6,282,950**	**41**	**1,849**	**10.1**	**7,213**	**124.4**
SuperSpeedways (2 miles or greater)																
California	2.0	4	2	50.0	3	3	1	8.8	4.3	0	463,765	3	287	28.7	665	166.3
Daytona	2.5	16	4	25.0	8	10	2	10.5	12.2	1	3,811,927	12	336	11.8	2,191	136.9
Indianapolis	2.5	7	2	28.6	4	5	3	8.9	12.1	1	3,276,076	6	277	24.7	981	140.1
Michigan	2.0	16	1	6.3	11	12	2	8.9	7.1	2	928,405	13	514	16.1	2,486	155.4
Pocono	2.5	16	3	18.8	8	12	2	7.6	9.8	2	1,069,235	12	574	17.9	2,338	146.1
Talladega	2.66	16	2	12.5	7	8	0	13.6	15.2	4	1,203,665	13	364	12.3	2,036	127.3
Totals		**75**	**14**	**18.7**	**41**	**50**	**10**	**9.9**	**10.8**	**10**	**$10,753,073**	**59**	**2,352**	**16.4**	**10,697**	**142.6**
Road Courses																
Sears Point	1.949	8	3	37.5	5	6	2	5.3	7.8	1	607,465	4	183	25.9	1,227	153.4
Watkins Glen	2.454	8	3	37.5	5	6	1	5.9	9.1	1	571,860	4	146	20.3	1,187	148.4
Totals		**16**	**6**	**37.5**	**10**	**12**	**3**	**5.6**	**8.4**	**2**	**$1,179,325**	**8**	**329**	**23.1**	**2,414**	**150.9**

Gordon settles into his car as his crew makes final pre-race adjustments. Since 1995, no driver has a better average start than Gordon. Over the last six seasons, Gordon has an average start of 7.9, followed by Mark Martin's 9.4.

Jeff Gordon's Standing in Winston Cup History—
All-Time and the Modern Era

In 1972, NASCAR history shifted abruptly to a new plateau. A series sponsorship deal with the R. J. Reynolds tobacco company ushered in the series' "Modern Era," changing the NASCAR world fundamentally. The most important change was a significant reduction in the number of races staged on a reduced number of racetracks. Accompanied by the 1975 introduction of the current point system, which rewards making the race and consistency more than victories, the result has been a steady increase in the series' competitiveness. Today, more teams show up every weekend with more race knowledge about fewer racetracks and with better funding from a more diverse set of sponsors than ever before.

From a statistical point of view, 1972 makes historical comparison a tap dance. Pitting Gordon's modern-era career against the cross-era career of a racer such as Richard Petty is fruitless. In 1967, Petty won 27 times in 48 starts. Often, he was one of just a few Grand National regulars to enter a race, giving him an enormous advantage over the local Saturday night racers against whom he competed. In 2001, 36 Winston Cup races are scheduled, the most since 46 were slated in 1971—the year before the modern era began.

In recognition of these distinct eras, this section puts Gordon's career in both contexts, All-Time and Modern Era. All-time records include all drivers who have competed since NASCAR's inception in 1949. The Modern Era includes only results beginning in 1972.

All-Time Records	29-31
Modern Era Records	32-35

Driving a Chevy Lumina in its final season of Winston Cup competition, Gordon won the inaugural Brickyard 400 at the famed Indianapolis Motor Speedway in 1994. A former resident of nearby Pittsboro, the 23-year-old "hometown boy" electrified the estimated crowd of 300,000 by surviving a late-race duel with Ernie Irvan and etching his name in history as the first stock-car winner in Indianapolis history.

All-Time Records

Championships

	Driver	
1	Dale Earnhardt	7
	Richard Petty	7
3	**Jeff Gordon**	**3**
	David Pearson	3
	Lee Petty	3
	Darrell Waltrip	3
	Cale Yarborough	3
8	Buck Baker	2
	Tim Flock	2
	Ned Jarrett	2
	Terry Labonte	2
	Herb Thomas	2
	Joe Weatherly	2
14	Bobby Allison	1
	Red Byron	1
	Bill Elliott	1
	Bobby Isaac	1
	Dale Jarrett	1
	Alan Kulwicki	1
	Bobby Labonte	1
	Benny Parsons	1
	Bill Rexford	1
	Rusty Wallace	1
	Rex White	1

Career Starts

	Driver	
1	Richard Petty	1,184
2	Dave Marcis	878
3	Darrell Waltrip	809
4	Bobby Allison	718
5	Buddy Baker	699
6	Ricky Rudd	695
7	Dale Earnhardt	675
8	Terry Labonte	673
9	J.D. McDuffie	653
10	Buck Baker	636
11	Bill Elliott	623
12	James Hylton	601
13	Kyle Petty	585
14	David Pearson	574
15	Buddy Arrington	560
16	Cale Yarborough	559
17	Geoffrey Bodine	552
18	Elmo Langley	536
19	Benny Parsons	526
	Rusty Wallace	526
21	Sterling Marlin	503
22	Neil Castles	497
23	Wendell Scott	495
24	Ken Schrader	492
25	Morgan Shepherd	481
26	Harry Gant	474
27	Michael Waltrip	462
28	Mark Martin	458
29	Jimmy Means	455
30	Cecil Gordon	450
31	Lee Petty	427
32	Dale Jarrett	423
33	Jim Paschal	422
34	G.C. Spencer	415
35	Brett Bodine	406
36	Lake Speed	402
37	Frank Warren	396
38	Henley Gray	374
39	Neil Bonnett	363
40	Dick Brooks	358
41	Derrike Cope	354
42	Ned Jarrett	352
43	Ed Negre	338
	Rick Mast	338
45	Jimmy Spencer	334
	Bobby Hillin Jr.	334
47	Jabe Thomas	322
48	John Sears	318
49	Junior Johnson	313
	Ernie Irvan	313
65	**Jeff Gordon**	**257**

Career Wins

	Driver	
1	Richard Petty	200
2	David Pearson	105
3	Bobby Allison	85
4	Darrell Waltrip	84
5	Cale Yarborough	83
6	Dale Earnhardt	76
7	Lee Petty	54
8	Rusty Wallace	53
9	**Jeff Gordon**	**52**
10	Junior Johnson	50
	Ned Jarrett	50
12	Herb Thomas	48
13	Buck Baker	46
14	Bill Elliott	40
15	Tim Flock	39
16	Bobby Isaac	37
17	Fireball Roberts	33
18	Mark Martin	32
19	Rex White	28
20	Fred Lorenzen	26
21	Jim Paschal	25
	Joe Weatherly	25
23	Dale Jarrett	24
24	Benny Parsons	21
	Jack Smith	21
	Terry Labonte	21
27	Ricky Rudd	20
	Speedy Thompson	20
29	Buddy Baker	19
	Davey Allison	19
	Fonty Flock	19
32	Geoffrey Bodine	18
	Harry Gant	18
	Neil Bonnett	18
35	Curtis Turner	17
	Marvin Panch	17
37	Bobby Labonte	16
38	Ernie Irvan	15
	Jeff Burton	15
40	Dick Hutcherson	14
	LeeRoy Yarbrough	14
42	Dick Rathmann	13
	Tim Richmond	13
44	Donnie Allison	10
45	Bob Welborn	9
	Cotton Owens	9
	Paul Goldsmith	9
	Tony Stewart	9
49	Kyle Petty	8
50	A.J. Foyt	7
	Darel Dieringer	7
	Jim Reed	7
	Marshall Teague	7

Winning Pct.

	Driver	
1	Herb Thomas	20.87
2	Tim Flock	20.86
3	**Jeff Gordon**	**20.23**
4	David Pearson	18.29
5	Richard Petty	16.89
6	Fred Lorenzen	16.46
7	Fireball Roberts	16.02
8	Junior Johnson	15.97
9	Cale Yarborough	14.85
10	Ned Jarrett	14.20
11	Dick Hutcherson	13.59
12	Lee Petty	12.65
13	Fonty Flock	12.34
14	Rex White	12.02
15	Bobby Isaac	12.01
16	Bobby Allison	11.84
17	Dale Earnhardt	11.26
18	Joe Weatherly	10.87
19	Darrell Waltrip	10.38
20	Dick Rathmann	10.16
21	Speedy Thompson	0.10
22	Rusty Wallace	10.08
23	Davey Allison	9.95
24	Curtis Turner	9.24
25	Jack Smith	7.98
26	Marvin Panch	7.87
27	Buck Baker	7.23
28	Paul Goldsmith	7.09
29	LeeRoy Yarbrough	7.07
30	Tim Richmond	7.03
31	Mark Martin	6.99
32	Jeff Burton	6.73
33	Jim Reed	6.60
34	Bill Elliott	6.42
35	Bobby Labonte	6.20
36	Jim Paschal	5.92
37	Dale Jarrett	5.67
38	Cotton Owens	5.63
39	A.J. Foyt	5.47
40	Neil Bonnett	4.96
41	Bob Welborn	4.92
42	Ernie Irvan	4.81
43	Donnie Allison	4.13
44	Benny Parsons	3.99
45	Darel Dieringer	3.87
46	Harry Gant	3.80
47	Geoffrey Bodine	3.26
48	Charlie Glotzbach	3.23
49	Terry Labonte	3.12
50	Ricky Rudd	2.88

All-Time Records

#	Career Money		#	Top 5s		#	Career Top 5 Pct.		#	Top 10s	
1	Dale Earnhardt	$41,176,756	1	Richard Petty	555	1	Dick Hutcherson	62.14	1	Richard Petty	712
2	**Jeff Gordon**	**34,571,265**	2	Bobby Allison	336	2	Tim Flock	54.55	2	Bobby Allison	446
3	Dale Jarrett	27,752,114	3	David Pearson	301	3	Lee Petty	54.10	3	Dale Earnhardt	428
4	Mark Martin	25,344,978	4	Dale Earnhardt	281	4	Dick Rathmann	53.91	4	Darrell Waltrip	390
5	Rusty Wallace	24,645,320	5	Darrell Waltrip	276	5	Herb Thomas	53.04	5	Buck Baker	372
6	Bill Elliott	23,636,122	6	Cale Yarborough	255	6	Ned Jarrett	52.56	6	David Pearson	366
7	Terry Labonte	23,505,569	7	Buck Baker	246	7	David Pearson	52.44	7	Mike Bliss	340
8	Darrell Waltrip	22,493,879	8	Lee Petty	231	**8**	**Jeff Gordon**	**50.19**	8	Terry Labonte	337
9	Bobby Labonte	20,846,605	9	Buddy Baker	202	9	Fred Lorenzen	47.47	9	Lee Petty	332
10	Ricky Rudd	19,603,630	10	Benny Parsons	199	10	Rex White	47.21	10	Ricky Rudd	322
11	Jeff Burton	17,961,877	11	Mark Martin	185	11	Richard Petty	46.88	11	Cale Yarborough	318
12	Ken Schrader	15,677,068		Ned Jarrett	185	12	Bobby Allison	46.80	12	Buddy Baker	311
13	Sterling Marlin	15,375,048	13	Terry Labonte	175	13	Fonty Flock	46.75	13	James Hylton	301
14	Geoffrey Bodine	14,747,014	14	Rusty Wallace	174	14	Joe Weatherly	45.65	14	Bill Elliott	285
15	Kyle Petty	12,322,649	15	Ricky Rudd	165	15	Cale Yarborough	45.62	15	Benny Parsons	283
16	Ernie Irvan	11,624,617	16	Bill Elliott	155	16	Fireball Roberts	45.15	16	Mark Martin	278
17	Bobby Hamilton	10,462,749	17	Jim Paschal	149	17	Marvin Panch	44.44		Rusty Wallace	278
18	Jimmy Spencer	10,079,244	18	James Hylton	140	18	Bobby Isaac	43.51	18	Ned Jarrett	239
19	Michael Waltrip	9,906,852	19	Bobby Isaac	134	19	Dale Earnhardt	41.63	19	Jim Paschal	230
20	Ward Burton	9,369,340	**20**	**Jeff Gordon**	**129**	20	Mark Martin	40.39	20	Dave Marcis	222
21	Jeremy Mayfield	8,952,218		Dale Jarrett	129	21	Speedy Thompson	39.39	21	Harry Gant	208
22	John Andretti	8,725,226	22	Harry Gant	123	22	Buck Baker	38.68	22	Elmo Langley	193
23	Morgan Shepherd	8,565,265	23	Herb Thomas	122	23	Junior Johnson	38.66	23	Dale Jarrett	191
24	Richard Petty	8,541,218	24	Junior Johnson	121	24	Benny Parsons	37.83	24	Geoffrey Bodine	188
25	Harry Gant	8,524,844	25	Rex White	110	25	Jim Reed	35.85	25	Neil Castles	178
26	Brett Bodine	8,403,254	26	Joe Weatherly	105	26	Jack Smith	35.74	26	Ken Schrader	171
27	Ted Musgrave	8,390,905	27	Tim Flock	102	27	Jim Paschal	35.31	27	Bobby Isaac	170
28	Rick Mast	8,079,728	28	Geoffrey Bodine	99	28	Paul Goldsmith	34.65	28	Kyle Petty	167
29	Bobby Allison	7,673,808	29	Marvin Panch	96	29	Davey Allison	34.55	**29**	**Jeff Gordon**	**166**
30	Joe Nemechek	7,348,729	30	Dave Marcis	94	30	Darrell Waltrip	34.12	30	Morgan Shepherd	165
31	Mike Skinner	7,220,956		Jack Smith	94	31	Rusty Wallace	33.08	31	Rex White	163
32	Dave Marcis	7,059,562	32	Fireball Roberts	93	32	LeeRoy Yarbrough	32.83	32	Sterling Marlin	158
33	Johnny Benson	6,960,014	33	Neil Bonnett	83	33	Jeff Burton	32.74	33	Herb Thomas	156
34	Tony Stewart	6,798,340	34	Donnie Allison	78	34	Cotton Owens	32.50		Neil Bonnett	156
35	Davey Allison	6,689,154		Speedy Thompson	78	35	Donnie Allison	32.23	35	Joe Weatherly	153
36	Kenny Wallace	6,338,106	36	Bobby Labonte	75	36	Bob Welborn	31.69	36	Dick Brooks	150
37	Wally Dallenbach Jr.	6,080,578		Fred Lorenzen	75	37	Charlie Glotzbach	30.65	37	Junior Johnson	148
38	Derrike Cope	6,022,678	38	Jeff Burton	73	38	Dale Jarrett	30.50	38	Wendell Scott	147
39	Chad Little	5,792,830	39	Fonty Flock	72	39	Curtis Turner	29.35	39	Jack Smith	141
40	Cale Yarborough	5,645,887	40	Dick Rathmann	69	40	Bobby Labonte	29.07	40	G.C. Spencer	138
41	Lake Speed	5,452,187	41	Ernie Irvan	68	41	Buddy Baker	28.90	41	Tim Flock	129
42	Dick Trickle	5,233,624	42	Davey Allison	66	42	Terry Labonte	26.00	42	John Sears	127
43	Robert Pressley	5,138,514	43	LeeRoy Yarbrough	65	43	Harry Gant	25.95	43	Marvin Panch	126
44	Alan Kulwicki	5,059,052	44	Dick Hutcherson	64	44	Bill Elliott	24.88	44	Bobby Labonte	122
45	Ricky Craven	4,820,585		Ken Schrader	64	45	Darel Dieringer	24.86		Fireball Roberts	122
46	Hut Stricklin	4,810,644	46	Elmo Langley	63	46	Bill Blair	24.39	46	Tiny Lund	119
47	Kenny Irwin	4,606,943	47	Morgan Shepherd	62	47	Ricky Rudd	23.74	47	Donnie Allison	115
48	Steve Park	4,599,262	48	Sterling Marlin	59	48	James Hylton	23.29	48	Cecil Gordon	111
49	Jerry Nadeau	4,492,310	49	Bob Welborn	58	49	Joe Eubanks	23.27	49	J.D. McDuffie	106
50	Benny Parsons	4,426,287	50	Dick Brooks	57	50	Neil Bonnett	22.87		Speedy Thompson	106

All-Time Records

Career Poles

1	Richard Petty	126
2	David Pearson	113
3	Cale Yarborough	70
4	Bobby Allison	59
4	Darrell Waltrip	59
6	Bobby Isaac	50
7	Bill Elliott	49
8	Junior Johnson	47
9	Buck Baker	44
10	Buddy Baker	40
11	Mark Martin	39
	Tim Flock	39
13	Herb Thomas	38
14	Geoffrey Bodine	37
15	Rex White	36
16	Fireball Roberts	35
	Ned Jarrett	35
	Rusty Wallace	35
19	**Jeff Gordon**	**33**
	Fonty Flock	33
	Fred Lorenzen	33
22	Ricky Rudd	26
	Terry Labonte	26
24	Alan Kulwicki	24
	Jack Smith	24
26	Ken Schrader	23
27	Dale Earnhardt	22
	Dick Hutcherson	22
29	Bobby Labonte	21
	Marvin Panch	21
31	Benny Parsons	20
	Neil Bonnett	20
33	Ernie Irvan	19
	Joe Weatherly	19
35	Donnie Allison	18
	Lee Petty	18
	Speedy Thompson	18
38	Curtis Turner	17
	Harry Gant	17
40	Dave Marcis	14
	Davey Allison	14
	Glen Wood	14
	Tim Richmond	14
44	Charlie Glotzbach	12
	Jim Paschal	12
46	Cotton Owens	11
	Dale Jarrett	11
	Darel Dieringer	11
49	A.J. Foyt	10
	Dick Rathmann	10
	LeeRoy Yarbrough	10
	Sterling Marlin	10

Laps Led

1	Richard Petty	52,194
2	Cale Yarborough	31,776
3	Bobby Allison	27,539
4	Dale Earnhardt	25,697
5	David Pearson	25,425
6	Darrell Waltrip	23,130
7	Rusty Wallace	17,719
8	Bobby Isaac	13,229
9	Junior Johnson	12,651
10	**Jeff Gordon**	**10,698**
11	Bill Elliott	10,324
12	Buddy Baker	9,748
13	Mark Martin	9,570
14	Ned Jarrett	9,468
15	Geoffrey Bodine	8,680
16	Harry Gant	8,445
17	Fred Lorenzen	8,131
18	Tim Flock	6,937
19	Ricky Rudd	6,872
20	Benny Parsons	6,860
21	Terry Labonte	6,807
22	Neil Bonnett	6,383
23	Herb Thomas	6,197
24	Dale Jarrett	6,004
25	Fireball Roberts	5,970
26	Buck Baker	5,662
27	Ernie Irvan	5,484
28	Davey Allison	4,991
29	Lee Petty	4,787
30	Curtis Turner	4,771
31	Fonty Flock	4,682
32	Donnie Allison	4,642
33	Jim Paschal	4,591
34	Rex White	4,583
35	Jeff Burton	4,169
36	Dick Hutcherson	3,995
37	Kyle Petty	3,847
38	Speedy Thompson	3,667
39	Joe Weatherly	3,487
40	LeeRoy Yarbrough	3,421
41	Jack Smith	3,228
42	Marvin Panch	3,089
43	Bobby Labonte	2,974
44	Sterling Marlin	2,799
45	Dave Marcis	2,699
46	Alan Kulwicki	2,686
47	Tim Richmond	2,537
48	Darel Dieringer	2,517
49	Tony Stewart	2,439
50	Ken Schrader	2,363

Races Led

1	Richard Petty	599
2	Bobby Allison	414
3	Dale Earnhardt	404
4	Darrell Waltrip	402
5	Cale Yarborough	340
6	David Pearson	329
7	Rusty Wallace	244
8	Buddy Baker	242
9	Terry Labonte	237
10	Bill Elliott	232
11	Mark Martin	228
12	Geoffrey Bodine	220
13	Ricky Rudd	196
14	Dave Marcis	195
15	Benny Parsons	192
	Harry Gant	192
17	**Jeff Gordon**	**176**
18	Bobby Isaac	155
	Neil Bonnett	155
20	Dale Jarrett	154
21	Junior Johnson	138
22	Ken Schrader	134
23	Ernie Irvan	123
24	Sterling Marlin	119
25	Bobby Labonte	113
26	Ned Jarrett	111
27	Donnie Allison	105
28	Morgan Shepherd	104
29	Buck Baker	103
30	Kyle Petty	98
31	Davey Allison	97
32	Lee Petty	93
33	Fireball Roberts	90
34	Herb Thomas	84
	Jeff Burton	84
36	Fred Lorenzen	83
37	Tim Flock	82
38	Michael Waltrip	78
39	Alan Kulwicki	77
40	Jim Paschal	76
	Tim Richmond	76
42	Curtis Turner	69
43	Joe Weatherly	67
44	LeeRoy Yarbrough	66
	Rex White	66
46	James Hylton	65
47	Jimmy Spencer	63
47	Marvin Panch	63
49	Brett Bodine	61
50	Fonty Flock	56

Modern Era Records

	Championships			Starts			Victories			Winning Pct.	
1	Dale Earnhardt	7	1	Darrell Waltrip	809	1	Darrell Waltrip	84	1	David Pearson	21.84
2	Richard Petty	4	2	Dave Marcis	756	2	Dale Earnhardt	76	**2**	**Jeff Gordon**	**20.23**
3	**Jeff Gordon**	**3**	3	Ricky Rudd	695	3	Cale Yarborough	69	3	Cale Yarborough	18.85
	Darrell Waltrip	3	4	Dale Earnhardt	675	4	Richard Petty	60	4	Mark Donohue	16.67
	Cale Yarborough	3	5	Terry Labonte	673	5	Bobby Allison	55	5	Tony Stewart	13.24
6	Terry Labonte	2	6	Bill Elliott	623	6	Rusty Wallace	53	6	Bobby Allison	11.55
7	Bobby Allison	1	7	Richard Petty	619	**7**	**Jeff Gordon**	**52**	7	Dale Earnhardt	11.26
	Bill Elliott	1	8	Kyle Petty	585	8	David Pearson	45	8	Darrell Waltrip	10.38
	Dale Jarrett	1	9	Geoffrey Bodine	552	9	Bill Elliott	40	9	Rusty Wallace	10.08
	Alan Kulwicki	1	10	Rusty Wallace	526	10	Mark Martin	32	10	Davey Allison	9.95
	Bobby Labonte	1	11	Sterling Marlin	503	11	Dale Jarrett	24	11	Richard Petty	9.69
	Benny Parsons	1	12	Ken Schrader	492	12	Terry Labonte	21	12	Tim Richmond	7.03
	Rusty Wallace	1	13	Morgan Shepherd	478	13	Ricky Rudd	20	13	Mark Martin	6.99
			14	Bobby Allison	476		Benny Parsons	20	14	Jeff Burton	6.73
			15	Harry Gant	474	15	Davey Allison	19	15	Bill Elliott	6.42
			16	Michael Waltrip	462	16	Neil Bonnett	18	16	Bobby Labonte	6.20
			17	Mark Martin	458		Geoffrey Bodine	18	17	Ray Elder	5.88
			18	Jimmy Means	455		Harry Gant	18	18	Dale Jarrett	5.67
			19	J.D. McDuffie	443	19	Bobby Labonte	16	19	Dale Earnhardt Jr.	5.13
			20	Benny Parsons	441	20	Buddy Baker	15	20	Neil Bonnett	4.96
			21	Buddy Arrington	426		Ernie Irvan	15	21	Ernie Irvan	4.79
			22	Dale Jarrett	423		Jeff Burton	15	22	Benny Parsons	4.54
			23	Brett Bodine	406	23	Tim Richmond	13	23	Earl Ross	3.85
			24	Lake Speed	402	24	Tony Stewart	9	24	Buddy Baker	3.84
			25	Buddy Baker	391	25	Kyle Petty	8	25	Harry Gant	3.80
			26	Cale Yarborough	366	26	Sterling Marlin	6	26	Geoffrey Bodine	3.26
			27	Neil Bonnett	363	27	Alan Kulwicki	5	27	Terry Labonte	3.12
			28	Derrike Cope	354		Dave Marcis	5	28	Ricky Rudd	2.88
			29	Rick Mast	338	29	Morgan Shepherd	4	29	Donnie Allison	2.52
			30	Bobby Hillin Jr.	334		Donnie Allison	4	30	Matt Kenseth	2.50
				Jimmy Spencer	334		Ken Schrader	4	31	Alan Kulwicki	2.42
			32	James Hylton	325	32	Bobby Hamilton	3	32	A.J. Foyt	2.38
			33	Ernie Irvan	313		Jeremy Mayfield	3	33	Bobby Isaac	1.54
			34	Bobby Hamilton	301	34	A.J. Foyt	2	34	Jeremy Mayfield	1.44
			35	Cecil Gordon	300		John Andretti	2	35	Kyle Petty	1.37
			36	Ted Musgrave	298		Ward Burton	2	36	Sterling Marlin	1.19
			37	Dick Trickle	297		Derrike Cope	2	37	Steve Park	1.11
			38	Hut Stricklin	284		Jimmy Spencer	2	38	Bobby Hamilton	1.00
			39	Dick Brooks	276		Dale Earnhardt Jr.	2	39	Jerry Nadeau	0.97
			40	Richard Childress	272				40	Ward Burton	0.93
			41	D.K. Ulrich	261				41	John Andretti	0.88
			42	Greg Sacks	258				42	Morgan Shepherd	0.84
			42	Bobby Labonte	258				43	Ken Schrader	0.81
			44	**Jeff Gordon**	**257**				44	Jody Ridley	0.71
			45	Frank Warren	239				45	Dave Marcis	0.66
			46	Lennie Pond	232				46	Ron Bouchard	0.63
			47	Tommy Gale	229				47	Jimmy Spencer	0.60
			48	John Andretti	227				48	Derrike Cope	0.56
			49	Wally Dallenbach Jr.	225				49	Phil Parsons	0.50
			50	Jeff Burton	223				50	Joe Nemechek	0.45

Modern Era Records

Money Won

1	Dale Earnhardt	$41,176,756
2	**Jeff Gordon**	**34,571,265**
3	Dale Jarrett	27,752,114
4	Mark Martin	25,344,978
5	Rusty Wallace	24,645,320
6	Bill Elliott	23,636,122
7	Terry Labonte	23,505,569
8	Darrell Waltrip	22,493,879
9	Bobby Labonte	20,846,605
10	Ricky Rudd	19,603,630
11	Jeff Burton	17,961,877
12	Ken Schrader	15,677,068
13	Sterling Marlin	15,375,048
14	Geoffrey Bodine	14,747,014
15	Kyle Petty	12,322,649
16	Ernie Irvan	11,624,617
17	Bobby Hamilton	10,462,749
18	Jimmy Spencer	10,079,244
19	Michael Waltrip	9,906,852
20	Ward Burton	9,369,340
21	Jeremy Mayfield	8,952,218
22	John Andretti	8,725,226
23	Morgan Shepherd	8,565,265
24	Harry Gant	8,524,844
25	Brett Bodine	8,403,254
26	Ted Musgrave	8,390,905
27	Rick Mast	8,079,728
28	Joe Nemechek	7,348,729
29	Mike Skinner	7,220,956
30	Johnny Benson	6,960,014
31	Tony Stewart	6,798,340
32	Davey Allison	6,689,154
33	Kenny Wallace	6,338,106
34	Wally Dallenbach Jr.	6,080,578
35	Derrike Cope	6,022,678
36	Chad Little	5,792,830
37	Lake Speed	5,452,187
38	Dick Trickle	5,233,624
39	Robert Pressley	5,138,514
40	Alan Kulwicki	5,059,052
41	Ricky Craven	4,820,585
42	Hut Stricklin	4,810,644
43	Kenny Irwin	4,606,943
44	Steve Park	4,599,262
45	Jerry Nadeau	4,492,310

Top 5s

1	Dale Earnhardt	281
2	Darrell Waltrip	276
3	Richard Petty	221
4	Bobby Allison	217
5	Cale Yarborough	197
6	Mark Martin	185
7	Terry Labonte	175
8	Rusty Wallace	174
9	Benny Parsons	172
10	Ricky Rudd	165
11	Bill Elliott	155
12	**Jeff Gordon**	**129**
	Dale Jarrett	129
14	Buddy Baker	128
15	Harry Gant	123
16	David Pearson	108
17	Geoffrey Bodine	99
18	Neil Bonnett	83
19	Bobby Labonte	75
	Dave Marcis	75
21	Jeff Burton	73
22	Ernie Irvan	68
23	Davey Allison	66
24	Ken Schrader	64
25	Morgan Shepherd	63
26	Sterling Marlin	59
27	Kyle Petty	51
28	Donnie Allison	42
	Tim Richmond	42
30	Lennie Pond	39
31	Alan Kulwicki	38
32	Dick Brooks	30
33	Jeremy Mayfield	28
34	Tony Stewart	24
35	Jimmy Spencer	22
36	Ted Musgrave	20
	Cecil Gordon	20
38	Ron Bouchard	19
	Joe Ruttman	19
40	Michael Waltrip	18
41	Bobby Hamilton	17
42	Lake Speed	16
	Bobby Isaac	16
	Brett Bodine	16
45	Ward Burton	15
	Dick Trickle	15
	James Hylton	15
48	A.J. Foyt	14
49	John Andretti	12
50	Mike Skinner	10
	Joe Millikan	10
	Phil Parsons	10

Top 5 Pct.

1	Cale Yarborough	53.83
2	David Pearson	52.43
3	**Jeff Gordon**	**50.19**
4	Bobby Unser	50.00
5	Bobby Allison	45.59
6	Dale Earnhardt	41.63
7	Ray Elder	41.18
8	Mark Martin	40.39
9	Benny Parsons	39.00
10	Fred Lorenzen	37.50
11	Richard Petty	35.70
12	Tony Stewart	35.29
13	Davey Allison	34.55
14	Darrell Waltrip	34.12
15	Rusty Wallace	33.08
16	Buddy Baker	32.74
17	Jeff Burton	32.74
18	Dale Jarrett	30.50
19	Bobby Labonte	29.07
20	LeeRoy Yarbrough	27.78
21	Donnie Allison	26.42
22	Terry Labonte	26.00
23	Harry Gant	25.95
24	Bill Elliott	24.88
25	Bobby Isaac	24.62
26	Ricky Rudd	23.74
27	Neil Bonnett	22.87
28	Tim Richmond	22.70
29	Ernie Irvan	21.73
30	Gary Bettenhausen	20.00
	Ron Fellows	20.00
32	Earl Ross	19.23
33	Alan Kulwicki	18.36
34	Geoffrey Bodine	17.93
35	Ramo Stott	17.39
36	Lennie Pond	16.81
37	A.J. Foyt	16.67
	Charlie Glotzbach	16.67
	Jim Insolo	16.67
	Mark Donohue	16.67
41	George Follmer	15.00
42	Carl Joiner	14.29
	Jackie Oliver	14.29
	Pete Hamilton	14.29
45	Jeremy Mayfield	13.40
46	Morgan Shepherd	13.18
47	Ken Schrader	13.01
48	Joe Millikan	12.50
48	Matt Kenseth	12.50
50	Ron Bouchard	11.88

Top 10s

1	Dale Earnhardt	428
2	Darrell Waltrip	390
3	Terry Labonte	337
4	Ricky Rudd	322
5	Richard Petty	311
6	Bobby Allison	300
7	Bill Elliott	285
8	Rusty Wallace	278
	Mark Martin	278
10	Benny Parsons	239
11	Cale Yarborough	231
12	Harry Gant	208
13	Buddy Baker	199
14	Dale Jarrett	191
15	Geoffrey Bodine	188
16	Dave Marcis	180
17	Ken Schrader	171
18	Morgan Shepherd	168
19	Kyle Petty	167
20	**Jeff Gordon**	**166**
21	Sterling Marlin	158
22	Neil Bonnett	156
23	Ernie Irvan	124
	David Pearson	124
25	Bobby Labonte	122
26	Dick Brooks	108
27	Jeff Burton	103
28	Davey Allison	92
29	Lennie Pond	88
30	James Hylton	87
31	Michael Waltrip	82
32	Tim Richmond	78
33	Richard Childress	76
34	Lake Speed	75
34	Alan Kulwicki	75
36	Cecil Gordon	71
37	Buddy Arrington	68
38	Donnie Allison	67
39	Jimmy Spencer	62
40	Ron Bouchard	60
41	Brett Bodine	59
	Joe Ruttman	59
43	Bobby Hamilton	57
	Ward Burton	57
45	Jody Ridley	56
46	Ted Musgrave	55
	J. D. McDuffie	55
48	Jeremy Mayfield	51
49	Tony Stewart	44
	Coo Coo Marlin	44

Modern Era Records

	Poles	
1	Darrell Waltrip	59
2	David Pearson	57
3	Cale Yarborough	51
4	Bill Elliott	49
5	Mark Martin	39
6	Geoffrey Bodine	37
7	Bobby Allison	36
8	Rusty Wallace	35
9	**Jeff Gordon**	**33**
10	Buddy Baker	30
11	Terry Labonte	26
	Ricky Rudd	26
13	Alan Kulwicki	24
14	Richard Petty	23
	Ken Schrader	23
16	Dale Earnhardt	22
	Ernie Irvan	22
18	Bobby Labonte	21
19	Neil Bonnett	20
20	Benny Parsons	19
21	Harry Gant	17
22	Tim Richmond	14
	Davey Allison	14
24	Dave Marcis	12
25	Dale Jarrett	11
26	Sterling Marlin	10
27	Donnie Allison	9
28	Bobby Isaac	8
	Kyle Petty	8
30	Morgan Shepherd	7
31	Jeremy Mayfield	6
	Joe Nemechek	6
	Ward Burton	6
34	Mike Skinner	5
	Brett Bodine	5
	Lennie Pond	5
	Ted Musgrave	5
	A.J. Foyt	5
	Bobby Hamilton	5
40	Tony Stewart	4
	Rick Mast	4
	John Andretti	4
43	Jeff Burton	3
	Joe Ruttman	3
	Kenny Irwin	3
	Loy Allen	3
	Ricky Craven	3
	Ron Bouchard	3
49	Greg Sacks	2
	Johnny Benson Jr.	2
	Dale Earnhardt Jr.	2
	Michael Waltrip	2
	Steve Park	2
	Kenny Wallace	2

	Laps Led	
1	Cale Yarborough	27,260
2	Dale Earnhardt	25,697
3	Darrell Waltrip	23,130
4	Bobby Allison	18,502
5	Rusty Wallace	17,719
6	Richard Petty	16,902
7	**Jeff Gordon**	**10,698**
8	Bill Elliott	10,324
9	David Pearson	10,079
10	Mark Martin	9,570
11	Geoffrey Bodine	8,680
12	Harry Gant	8,445
13	Ricky Rudd	6,872
14	Terry Labonte	6,807
15	Buddy Baker	6,580
16	Benny Parsons	6,552
17	Neil Bonnett	6,383
18	Dale Jarrett	6,004
19	Ernie Irvan	5,484
20	Davey Allison	4,991
21	Jeff Burton	4,169
22	Kyle Petty	3,847
23	Bobby Labonte	2,974
24	Sterling Marlin	2,799
25	Alan Kulwicki	2,686
26	Tim Richmond	2,537
27	Tony Stewart	2,439
28	Ken Schrader	2,363
29	Dave Marcis	2,332
30	Donnie Allison	2,297
31	Morgan Shepherd	2,141
32	Bobby Hamilton	1,736
33	Jeremy Mayfield	1,637
34	Bobby Isaac	1,399
35	Ward Burton	1,313
36	Brett Bodine	1,034
37	Mike Skinner	970
38	Lennie Pond	926
39	Jimmy Spencer	886
40	Joe Ruttman	807
41	A.J. Foyt	730
42	John Andretti	668
43	Lake Speed	632
44	Michael Waltrip	519
45	Ricky Craven	506
46	Rick Mast	478
47	Hut Stricklin	471
48	Steve Park	455
49	Dick Brooks	453
50	Dale Earnhardt Jr.	427

	Races Led	
1	Dale Earnhardt	404
2	Darrell Waltrip	402
3	Bobby Allison	306
4	Richard Petty	289
5	Cale Yarborough	271
6	Rusty Wallace	244
7	Terry Labonte	237
8	Bill Elliott	232
9	Mark Martin	227
10	Geoffrey Bodine	220
11	Ricky Rudd	196
12	Harry Gant	192
13	Dave Marcis	183
14	Benny Parsons	182
15	Buddy Baker	178
16	**Jeff Gordon**	**176**
17	Neil Bonnett	155
18	Dale Jarrett	154
19	David Pearson	140
20	Ken Schrader	133
21	Ernie Irvan	124
22	Sterling Marlin	120
23	Bobby Labonte	113
24	Morgan Shepherd	104
25	Kyle Petty	98
26	Davey Allison	97
27	Jeff Burton	84
28	Michael Waltrip	77
	Alan Kulwicki	77
30	Tim Richmond	76
31	Donnie Allison	69
32	Jimmy Spencer	63
33	Brett Bodine	61
34	Lennie Pond	53
35	Ward Burton	48
36	Bobby Hamilton	47
37	Jeremy Mayfield	46
38	John Andretti	44
39	Mike Skinner	40
40	Lake Speed	39
41	Ted Musgrave	38
42	Joe Ruttman	34
43	A.J. Foyt	33
	Tony Stewart	33
45	Bobby Isaac	31
46	James Hylton	29
	Johnny Benson Jr.	29
	Rick Mast	29
49	Ricky Craven	28
	Dick Brooks	28

	Average Start	
1	David Pearson	5.58
2	Cale Yarborough	7.15
3	Bobby Allison	8.44
4	**Jeff Gordon**	**8.81**
5	Benny Parsons	9.05
6	Mark Martin	9.38
7	Donnie Allison	9.97
8	Buddy Baker	10.73
9	Neil Bonnett	11.93
10	Alan Kulwicki	12.00
11	Davey Allison	12.38
12	Rusty Wallace	12.43
13	Tim Richmond	12.46
14	Harry Gant	12.51
15	Dale Earnhardt	12.91
16	Bill Elliott	13.09
17	Geoffrey Bodine	13.29
18	Richard Petty	13.40
19	Ricky Rudd	13.61
20	Darrell Waltrip	13.71
21	Bobby Labonte	14.22
22	Terry Labonte	14.52
23	Ken Schrader	14.84
24	Coo Coo Marlin	15.04
25	Ron Bouchard	15.12
26	Lennie Pond	15.43
27	Dick Brooks	15.92
28	Ernie Irvan	16.21
29	Dale Jarrett	16.88
30	Joe Ruttman	17.39
31	Morgan Shepherd	17.96
32	Mike Skinner	18.06
33	Sterling Marlin	18.14
34	Richard Childress	18.43
35	Jody Ridley	18.53
36	Ward Burton	18.55
37	Joe Nemechek	18.99
38	Brett Bodine	19.56
39	Rick Wilson	19.74
40	Kyle Petty	20.02
41	Jerry Nadeau	20.64
42	Jeff Burton	20.65
43	John Andretti	20.83
44	Walter Ballard	21.02
45	Lake Speed	21.13
46	Rick Mast	21.16
47	Michael Waltrip	21.32
48	Phil Parsons	21.35
49	Dave Marcis	21.60
50	Jeremy Mayfield	21.76

Modern Era Records

Average Finish

1	Dale Earnhardt	11.06
2	Cale Yarborough	11.45
3	Bobby Allison	11.58
4	**Jeff Gordon**	**11.72**
5	Mark Martin	12.33
6	David Pearson	13.45
7	Rusty Wallace	14.03
8	Richard Petty	14.15
9	Terry Labonte	14.23
10	Davey Allison	14.25
11	Benny Parsons	14.39
12	Bill Elliott	14.45
13	Bobby Labonte	14.87
14	Darrell Waltrip	15.12
15	Tim Richmond	15.18
16	Ricky Rudd	15.49
17	Buddy Baker	15.52
18	Dale Jarrett	15.64
19	Jeff Burton	15.83
20	Harry Gant	15.87
21	Alan Kulwicki	16.41
22	Neil Bonnett	16.52
23	Jody Ridley	16.58
24	Ken Schrader	16.88
25	Richard Childress	17.21
26	Ron Bouchard	17.23
27	James Hylton	17.34
28	Ernie Irvan	17.35
29	Lennie Pond	17.78
30	Dick Brooks	17.80
31	Buddy Arrington	17.84
32	Cecil Gordon	17.84
33	Sterling Marlin	17.91
34	Geoffrey Bodine	18.03
35	Elmo Langley	18.12
36	Morgan Shepherd	18.24
37	David Sisco	18.53
38	Donnie Allison	18.67
39	Kyle Petty	18.72
40	Walter Ballard	18.88
41	Coo Coo Marlin	19.05
42	Ted Musgrave	20.02
43	Frank Warren	20.08
44	Phil Parsons	20.12
45	Joe Ruttman	20.18
46	Jeremy Mayfield	20.44
47	Michael Waltrip	20.47
48	D. K. Ulrich	20.49
49	Dave Marcis	20.52
50	Mike Skinner	20.58

Gordon talks with Rick Mast (right) and Geoffrey Bodine (left) prior to the inaugural Brickyard in 1994. The three drivers were about to make indelible marks on the first-ever stock car race at Indianapolis. Gordon became the first winner of an Indy stock-car race, while Mast was the first Winston Cup pole winner at the track. Bodine, meanwhile, added drama to the race by trading on-track bumps with his brother, Brett. Their family feud culminated in a lap-100 wreck that knocked Geoffrey out of the race. Brett finished an impressive second to Gordon.

The Dupont crew tends to the No. 24 Chevy on pit road at Rockingham in 1998. In 16 races at "The Rock," Gordon has started outside of the Top 10 just twice. He has four wins at the track.

Chapter 3

A Season-by-Season Look at Jeff Gordon's Career

This section gets into the details of Gordon's career, allowing the reader to review his development season-by-season. Every race in Gordon's career is listed, presenting his start, finish, total laps, laps completed, race-ending condition, and money won. Also listed is Gordon's championship performance, including championship and bonus points earned for each race, his position in the points standings, and how far he trailed the points leader. If Gordon is the points leader at any point, the second-place driver in the standings is listed in parentheses along with the margin of Gordon's lead. The context of each race is also available with the "Career Race" column, which indicates the number of races in which Gordon had competed at any point in his career.

Each season is put into historical context with the inclusion of full statistics and a season summary. For each year, 20 statistical categories are cataloged. Gordon's total for each category is listed, along with his rank and that category's leader. If Gordon is the leader in a category, the second-place driver is listed in parentheses with his total. The season summary explores Gordon's accomplishments or details memorable moments and is often accompanied by tables that allow greater insight into his career.

Jeff Gordon and the Rainbow Warriors have been consistent, but not victorious at the Dura-Lube 500 held at Phoenix International Raceway. Gordon has posted 6 top 10 finishes since 1993, but he hasn't cracked the top three. Shown here in the 1998 race, Gordon finished on the lead lap in seventh place. *Nigel Kinrade*

Gordon precisely guides his 2001 Chevy Monte Carlo around New Hampshire International Raceway for the New England 300?a race in which Jeff Gordon battled with championship rival Dale Jarrett for the win. *Nigel Kinrade*

"They're capable of winning races when they're not the best car. We've seen that not just this year but in a number of years. It's uncanny."
—Dale Jarrett, Winston Cup driver, *Sport Magazine*

1993: Rookie of the Year

Jeff Gordon wasted little time in making a lasting impression as a rookie sensation in 1993. In the first race of his rookie campaign, the first Twin 125 qualifying race for the Daytona 500, the 21-year-old Gordon slipped past Bill Elliott on Lap 21 and led the final 29 laps en route to a historic victory. With the win, Gordon became the first rookie to win a Daytona 500 qualifying race in 30 years (Johnny Rutherford won in 1963) and the only rookie 125 winner in NASCAR's modern era. Building on his impressive start, Gordon followed up by leading the first lap of the Daytona 500 and finishing the race in fifth.

Of course, Gordon's rookie campaign wasn't pain-free. In fact, when compared to other top rookie seasons (see the accompanying chart), his first season looks less spectacular. He did not win a race or finish impressively in the point standings (Gordon ended 1993 in 14th place). Indeed, the rookie campaigns of Dale Earnhardt (senior and junior), Davey Allison, Tony Stewart, and Matt Kenseth—even Jody Ridley and Joe Millikan—can all be called more impressive than Gordon's.

One of the most telling stats of Gordon's rookie season is his series-leading 11 DNFs (Did Not Finish). Learning how to handle the heavier, more powerful Winston Cup cars, and how to handle his more experienced competitors, took a toll on the driver. The symbol of Gordon's rookie learning curve was North Wilkesboro, where he finished 34th—dead last—twice due to early crashes.

Despite these struggles, Gordon's season stands out because of the impression he made in the first week of the season. After Daytona, Gordon continued his strong start with solid runs in two of the next three races—sixth at Richmond and fourth at Atlanta. After the first four races of 1993, Gordon found himself in fifth in the championship points standings and the focus of the Winston Cup world. At season's end, Gordon earned the 1993 Rookie of the Year award, besting Bobby Labonte and Kenny Wallace.

Rookie Season Comparison

Driver	Year	Wins	Top 5s	Top 10s	Poles	Laps Led	Points Ranking	Money
Tony Stewart	1999	3	12	21	2	1,227	4th	$3,190,149
Davey Allison	1987	2	9	10	5	710	21st	361,060
Dale Earnhardt Jr.	2000	2	3	5	2	426	16th	2,793,596
Dale Earnhardt	1979	1	11	17	4	604	7th	274,810
Morgan Shepherd	1981	1	3	7	1	518	13th	170,473
Matt Kenseth	2000	1	4	11	0	162	14th	2,345,564
Joe Millikan	1979	0	5	20	1	188	6th	229,713
Jody Ridley	1980	0	2	18	0	2	7th	204,883
Jeff Gordon	1993	0	7	11	1	230	14th	765,168

Jeff Gordon and Bobby Labonte entered the Winston Cup series full time in 1993. Gordon achieved success more quickly, winning the 1993 Rookie of the Year award and Winston Cup titles in 1995, 1997, and 1998. Labonte emerged later with a dominating performance to win the championship in 2000.

Gordon in 1993

Category	Total	Rank	1993 Leader*
Money	$765,168	12th	Dale Earnhardt—3,353,789
Total Points	3,447	14th	Dale Earnhardt—4,526
Avg. Start	13.1	10th	Ernie Irvan—7.7
Avg. Finish	17.7	15th	Dale Earnhardt—8.2
Wins	0	—	Rusty Wallace—10
Top 5s	7	9th	Rusty Wallace—19
Top 10s	11	12th	Earnhardt, R. Wallace—21
DNFs	11	1st	(J. Horton, E. Irvan—10)
Poles	1	8th	Ken Schrader—6
Front Row Starts	1	12th	Ernie Irvan—9
Laps Led	230	11th	Rusty Wallace—2,860
Races Led	14	6th	Dale Earnhardt—21
Times Led	24	8th	Dale Earnhardt—81
Miles Led	303	10th	Dale Earnhardt—2,485
Times Led Most Laps	0	—	Earnhardt, R. Wallace—9
Bonus Points	70	6th	Dale Earnhardt—150
Laps Completed	8,390	23rd	Dale Earnhardt—9,787
Miles Completed	10,066	23rd	Dale Earnhardt—11,808
Points per Race	114.9	15th	Dale Earnhardt—150.9
Fin. on Lead Lap	11	8th	Rusty Wallace—23

* Second-place driver listed in parentheses if Gordon is category leader.

1993 Performance Chart
No. 24 Hendrick Motorsports Chevrolet

Career Race	Race No.	Date	Race	St.	Fin.	Total Laps	Laps Completed	Laps Led	Condition	Money	Pts.	Bonus Pts.	Point Standing	Behind Leader	Points Leader
2	1	Feb 14	Daytona—Daytona 500 by STP	3	5	200	200	2	Running	$111,150	160	5	5	-20	Earnhardt
3	2	Feb 28	Rockingham—GM Goodwrench 500	28	34	492	402	0	DNF—Engine	6,700	61	0	16	-134	Earnhardt
4	3	Mar 7	Richmond—Pontiac Excitement 400	8	6	400	400	0	Running	14,700	150	0	10	-119	Jarrett
5	4	Mar 20	Atlanta—Motorcraft Quality Parts 500	4	4	328	327	54	Running	32,000	165	5	5	-83	Earnhardt
6	5	Mar 28	Darlington—TranSouth 500	5	24	367	275	1	DNF—Mechanical	7,740	96	5	8	-172	Earnhardt
7	6	Apr 4	Bristol—Food City 500	21	17	500	481	0	DNF—Crash	9,400	112	0	9	-235	Earnhardt
8	7	Apr 18	North Wilkesboro—First Union 400	7	34	400	25	0	DNF—Crash	4,180	61	0	16	-307	R. Wallace
9	8	Apr 25	Martinsville—Hanes 500	3	8	500	497	0	Running	11,975	142	0	12	-350	R. Wallace
10	9	May 2	Talladega—Winston 500	30	11	188	188	0	Running	15,795	130	0	11	-375	R. Wallace
11	10	May 16	Sears Point—Save Mart Supermarket 300K	15	11	74	74	0	Running	10,215	130	0	10	-319	Earnhardt
12	11	May 30	Charlotte—Coca-Cola 600	21	2	400	400	3	Running	79,050	175	5	9	-329	Earnhardt
13	12	Jun 6	Dover—Budweiser 500	21	18	500	440	0	Running	11,485	109	0	10	-405	Earnhardt
14	13	Jun 13	Pocono—Champion Spark Plug 500	4	28	200	113	0	Running	8,535	79	0	10	-461	Earnhardt
15	14	Jun 20	Michigan—Miller Genuine Draft 400	23	2	200	200	2	Running	44,915	175	5	10	-412	Earnhardt
16	15	Jul 3	Daytona—Pepsi 400	27	5	160	160	3	Running	24,625	160	5	8	-437	Earnhardt
17	16	Jul 11	New Hampshire—Slick 50 300	3	7	300	300	3	Running	19,150	151	5	7	-371	Earnhardt
18	17	Jul 18	Pocono—Miller Genuine Draft 500	20	37	200	49	0	DNF—Engine	9,615	52	0	8	-504	Earnhardt
19	18	Jul 25	Talladega—DieHard 500	8	31	188	148	7	DNF—Engine	11,250	75	5	10	-614	Earnhardt
20	19	Aug 8	Watkins Glen—Bud at the Glen	11	31	90	64	0	DNF— Engine	7,290	70	0	10	-658	Earnhardt
21	20	Aug 15	Michigan—Champion Spark Plug 400	9	3	200	200	17	Running	34,745	170	5	10	-626	Earnhardt
22	21	Aug 28	Bristol—Bud 500[1]	8	20	500	466	0	Running	11,450	103	0	10	-688	Earnhardt
23	22	Sept 5	Darlington—Mountain Dew Southern 500	15	22	351	346	3	Running	8,870	102	5	10	-751	Earnhardt
24	23	Sept 11	Richmond—Miller Genuine Draft 400	22	10	400	400	0	Running	14,205	134	0	9	-782	Earnhardt
25	24	Sept 19	Dover—SplitFire Spark Plug 500	3	24	500	412	80	DNF—Mechanical	11,255	96	5	9	-768	Earnhardt
26	25	Sept 26	Martinsville—Goody's 500	25	11	500	498	0	Running	13,360	130	0	10	-714	Earnhardt
27	26	Oct 3	North Wilkesboro—Tyson/Holly Farms 400	16	34	400	117	0	DNF—Mechanical	5,655	61	0	11	-828	Earnhardt
28	27	Oct 10	Charlotte—Mello Yello 500	1	5	334	334	1	Running	56,875	160	5	10	-838	Earnhardt
29	28	Oct 24	Rockingham—AC Delco 500	7	21	492	486	0	Running	11,350	100	0	11	-913	Earnhardt
30	29	Oct 31	Phoenix—Slick 50 500	9	35	312	195	48	DNF—Mechanical	7,610	63	5	13	-1,015	Earnhardt
31	30	Nov 14	Atlanta—Hooters 500	15	31	328	193	6	DNF—Crash	8,710	75	5	14	-1,079	Earnhardt

[1] — Relieved by Todd Bodine

1994: Becoming 'Big Money'

Steady improvement and a developing reputation for being a "big-money" racer marked Jeff Gordon's second season on the Winston Cup circuit. Much like his rookie season, his achievements cannot be called historic, but his ability to shine in the series' biggest events overshadowed any struggles.

To be sure, Gordon's improvement in 1994 was significant. He made a considerable leap in the driver point standings (jumping to 8th after finishing 14th in his rookie season). He saw increases in wins, Top-10 finishes, laps led, bonus points, prize winnings, and races led. Gordon also saw solid improvements in his average starting and finishing positions. Still, considering Dale Earnhardt won a championship in his second season and Tony Stewart broke out with a series-leading six wins in his second go-around, Gordon's sophomore performance can hardly be called earth shattering. For instance, despite his improved performance, Gordon was still among the series leaders in DNFs and actually saw his lead-lap finishes decrease from his rookie season.

Forever causing amnesia about Gordon's sophomore struggles, however, will be his first two career victories in the Coca-Cola 600 and the inaugural Brickyard 400.

As the biggest race of the season (even outshining that season's Daytona 500), the 1994 Brickyard 400 represents Gordon's arrival as a NASCAR star. When the big race and the big money were on the line—the Brickyard's purse was a then-record $2,687,249—Gordon emerged.

A former resident of nearby Pittsboro, Indiana (a town just 14 miles from the Speedway), Gordon led the most laps in a race for the first time (leading 93 of the Brickyard's 160 laps) and held his own in a classic duel with Ernie Irvan as the race expired. With four laps remaining, Irvan suffered a cut tire, opening the door for the hometown boy's victory.

Another telling and prescient moment earlier in 1994 was Gordon's first-ever Winston Cup victory in the Coca-Cola 600 at Charlotte. Though Rusty Wallace dominated the race, the 600 marked the first indication of the kind of team Gordon and his crew chief Ray Evernham were becoming. With 19 laps remaining, they agreed to take just two tires during their last green-flag pit stop, a choice that contradicted the four-tire stops of the other leaders. The two-tire decision allowed Gordon to complete his pit stop in half the time of the other leaders and go on to win the race.

The Coca-Cola 600 and Brickyard victories gave Gordon two of the season's three biggest paydays—$613,000 at Indy and $196,000 at Charlotte. Gordon was becoming big money.

Gordon in 1994

Category	Total	Rank	1994 Leader
Money	$1,779,523	3rd	Dale Earnhardt—3,300,733
Total Points	3,776	8th	Dale Earnhardt—4,694
Avg. Start	9.8	3rd	Ernie Irvan—6.6
Avg. Finish	15.8	10th	Dale Earnhardt—8.0
Wins	2	6th	Rusty Wallace—8
Top 5s	7	7th	Dale Earnhardt—20
Top 10s	14	8th	Dale Earnhardt—25
DNFs	10	6th	Geoffrey Bodine—15
Poles	1	7th	G. Bodine, E. Irvan—5
Front Row Starts	2	9th	Geoffrey Bodine—10
Laps Led	446	7th	Rusty Wallace—2,142
Races Led	17	5th	Dale Earnhardt—23
Times Led	38	6th	Ernie Irvan—79
Miles Led	658	6th	Ernie Irvan—2,419
Times Led Most Laps	1	7th	Ernie Irvan—10
Bonus Points	90	8th	Ernie Irvan—135
Laps Completed	9,277	9th	Darrell Waltrip—9,905
Miles Completed	11,548	6th	Ricky Rudd—12,046
Points per Race	121.8	9th	Ernie Irvan—151.3
Fin. on Lead Lap	10	10th	Dale Earnhardt—22

1994 Performance Chart
No. 24 Hendrick Motorsports Chevrolet

Career Race	Race No.	Date	Race	St.	Total Fin.	Total Laps	Laps Completed	Led	Condition	Money	Bonus Pts.	Point Pts.	Behind Standing	Points Leader	Leader
32	1	Feb 20	Daytona — Daytona 500	6	4	200	200	7	Running	$112,525	165	5	4	-15	Marlin
33	2	Feb 27	Rockingham — Goodwrench 500	3	32	492	462	0	DNF— Crash	13,500	67	0	11	-123	Marlin
34	3	Mar 6	Richmond — Pontiac Excitement 400	8	3	400	400	2	Running	34,000	170	5	6	-118	Irvan
35	4	Mar 13	Atlanta — Purolator 500	17	8	328	326	0	Running	21,550	142	0	7	-161	Irvan
36	5	Mar 27	Darlington — TranSouth Financial 400	13	31	293	236	0	DNF— Engine	11,745	70	0	9	-246	Irvan
37	6	Apr 10	Bristol — Food City 500	4	22	500	425	68	DNF— Crash	14,855	102	5	9	-248	Earnhardt
38	7	Apr 17	North Wilkesboro — First Union 400	12	15	400	396	0	Running	13,100	118	0	12	-285	Earnhardt
39	8	Apr 24	Martinsville — Hanes 500	13	33	500	394	0	Running	10,475	64	0	14	-376	Irvan
40	9	May 1	Talladega — Winston Select 500	40	24	188	184	3	Running	15,525	96	5	15	-460	Irvan
41	10	May 15	Sears Point — Save Mart Supermarkets 300	6	37	74	59	0	DNF— Rear End	12,675	52	0	18	-593	Irvan
42	11	May 29	Charlotte — Coca-Cola 600	1	1	400	400	16	Running	196,500	180	5	13	-573	Irvan
43	12	Jun 5	Dover — Budweiser 500	23	5	500	500	0	Running	33,570	155	0	12	-598	Irvan
44	13	Jun 12	Pocono — UAW-GM Teamwork 500	4	6	200	200	2	Running	23,505	155	5	11	-594	Irvan
45	14	Jun 19	Michigan — Miller Genuine Draft 400	7	12	200	200	62	Running	22,175	132	5	9	-576	Irvan
46	15	Jul 2	Daytona — Pepsi 400	12	8	160	160	19	Running	25,175	147	5	9	-609	Irvan
47	16	Jul 10	New Hampshire — Slick 50 300	2	39	300	160	9	DNF— Crash	22,100	51	5	10	-645	Earnhardt
48	17	Jul 17	Pocono — Miller Genuine Draft 500	7	8	200	199	0	Running	21,760	142	0	9	-649	Earnhardt
49	18	Jul 24	Talladega — DieHard 500	15	31	188	149	0	DNF— Engine	19,660	70	0	10	-661	Irvan
50	19	Aug 6	Indianapolis — Brickyard 400	3	1	160	160	93	Running	613,000	185	10	9	-620	Earnhardt
51	20	Aug 14	Watkins Glen — The Bud at the Glen	3	9	90	90	0	Running	19,950	138	0	8	-652	Earnhardt
52	21	Aug 21	Michigan — GM Goodwrench Dealer 400	3	15	200	198	8	DNF— Engine	21,565	123	5	8	-581	Earnhardt
53	22	Aug 27	Bristol — Goody's 500	12	32	500	222	36	DNF— Crash	17,735	72	5	9	-679	Earnhardt
54	23	Sept 4	Darlington — Mountain Dew Southern 500	7	6	367	366	0	Running	22,765	150	0	9	-704	Earnhardt
55	24	Sept 10	Richmond — Miller Genuine Draft 400	13	2	400	400	2	Running	40,365	175	5	8	-699	Earnhardt
56	25	Sept 18	Dover — SplitFire Spark Plug 500	12	11	500	499	0	Running	20,615	130	0	7	-744	Earnhardt
57	26	Sept 25	Martinsville — Goody's 500	6	11	500	499	14	Running	19,810	135	5	7	-784	Earnhardt
58	27	Oct 2	North Wilkesboro — Tyson Holly Farms 400	12	8	400	398	0	Running	16,875	142	0	7	-793	Earnhardt
59	28	Oct 9	Charlotte — Mello Yello 500	5	28	334	324	3	DNF— Crash	16,730	84	5	7	-879	Earnhardt
60	29	Oct 23	Rockingham — AC Delco 500	15	29	492	437	101	DNF— Mechanical	26,300	81	5	9	-983	Earnhardt
61	30	Oct 30	Phoenix — Slick 50 500	14	4	312	311	1	Running	26,780	165	5	8	-861	Earnhardt
62	31	Nov 13	Atlanta — Hooters 500	6	15	328	323	0	Running	20,125	118	0	8	-918	Earnhardt

"The truly great drivers—A.J., Gurney, Donohue, Andretti—all proved themselves in a variety of race cars. Unless Jeff steps into Indy cars or Formula 1, he'll forever be considered a great stock-car driver, but not one of the greats."
—Chris Economaki, auto racing journalist, *Road and Track*

Though Bristol would later become one of Jeff Gordon's best tracks, in 1994 it was a nightmare for the young driver. He suffered race-ending wrecks in both 1994 Bristol events, finishing 22nd in the spring race and 36th in the August night race. *Jennifer Regruth*

Gordon passes Ernie Irvan's No. 28 Texaco-Havoline Ford in late-race action during the inaugural Brickyard 400 in 1994. Gordon and Irvan's classic duel late in the race ended prematurely when a cut tire forced Irvan, who finished 17th, to pit with just four laps remaining. His most serious challenger out of contention, Gordon went on to a comfortable five-car length victory.

"Can he do what Muhammed Ali and [Michael] Jordan did and go beyond his sport? He might, because he's the antithesis of what a racer should be. He's not a good ol' tobacco-chewing guy. But he needs what Ali and Arnold Palmer had—great victories over tremendous competition. Now, he makes it look too easy."
—Humpy Wheeler, Charlotte Motor Speedway president, *Fortune*

1995: The First Championship

If steady improvement and reputation building marked Jeff Gordon's second season on the Winston Cup circuit, 1995 was the year he broke through. Gordon made history in his third season. He was aided by the re-introduction of Chevrolet's dominant Monte Carlo (which won 25 of the season's 35 races, including the Busch Clash, both Twin 125s and the Winston Select).

At age 24, Gordon became the youngest driver to win the Winston Cup since the 23-year-old Bill Rexford won in 1950 (see the accompanying chart). In accumulating $4,347,343 in winnings, he easily shattered the previous money record and became the first driver ever to exceed the $4 million plateau. His reputation as a "big-money" racer solidified.

The extent of the step-change in Gordon's performance in 1995 was breathtaking. Though he would assemble amazing seasons in 1996, 1997, and 1998, in some ways 1995 was Gordon's most dominant season, particularly in putting his No. 24 Chevy in the lead and keeping it there. Gordon led 29 of 31 races in 1995, the second highest total in the Modern Era. He led 2,600 of the season's 9,863 laps, the 15th-best effort in the Modern Era. Translated, he led one of every four laps in 1995.

As it turned out, Gordon's propensity to lead early and often—he led the most laps 11 times—was an integral part of his championship run. His 200 bonus points helped him overcome the fact that Dale Earnhardt actually had the season's best average finish (9.2 vs. Gordon's 9.5). By the end of the season, Gordon found he needed every one of those bonus points. Shrugging off a handful of poor finishes early in the season, Gordon reeled off 14 straight Top-8 finishes (including four wins) to build a 302-point lead on Earnhardt heading into the final four races of the year.

But finishes by Gordon of 30th, 20th, 5th, and 32nd in the final four races allowed Earnhardt (who finished 2nd, 7th, 3rd, and 1st in the same span) to close quickly in the standings. Gordon eventually won by just 34 points, the eighth closest points race in Winston Cup history.

In addition to his first championship, Gordon continued to build his impressive racing resume. His seven victories led the series and included his first Southern 500 title. His eight poles were the highest total in 10 seasons.

Gordon in 1995

Category	Total	Rank	1995 Leader*
Money	$4,347,343	1st	(Dale Earnhardt—3,154,241)
Total Points	4,614	1st	(Dale Earnhardt—4,580)
Avg. Start	5.0	1st	(Mark Martin—8.4)
Avg. Finish	9.5	2nd	Dale Earnhardt—9.2
Wins	7	1st	(Dale Earnhardt—5)
Top 5s	17	2nd	Dale Earnhardt—19
Top 10s	23	T-1st	(Dale Earnhardt—23)
DNFs	3	29th	G. Sacks, D. Waltrip—11
Poles	8	1st	(Mark Martin—4)
Front Row Starts	12	1st	(M. Martin, R. Rudd—7)
Laps Led	2,600	1st	(Dale Earnhardt—1,583)
Races Led	29	1st	(Dale Earnhardt—24)
Times Led	94	1st	(Dale Earnhardt—71)
Miles Led	3,458	1st	(Dale Earnhardt—1,739)
Times Led Most Laps	11	1st	(Earnhardt, Martin—4)
Bonus Points	200	1st	(Dale Earnhardt—140)
Laps Completed	9,405	6th	Sterling Marlin—9,728
Miles Completed	11,608	4th	Sterling Marlin—11,936
Points per Race	148.8	1st	(Dale Earnhardt—147.7)
Fin. on Lead Lap	23	1st	(Dale Earnhardt—22)

* Second-place driver or co-leader listed in parentheses if Gordon is category leader.

Youngest Champions

Driver	Title Year	Age
Bill Rexford	1950	23 years, 229 days
Jeff Gordon	1995	24 years, 100 days
Richard Petty	1964	27 years, 129 days
Terry Labonte	1984	28 years, 2 days
Tim Flock	1952	28 years, 203 days
Herb Thomas	1951	28 years, 234 days

1995 Performance Chart
No. 24 Hendrick Motorsports Chevrolet

Career Race	Race No.	Date	Race	St.	Fin.	Total Laps	Laps Completed	Laps Led	Condition	Money	Pts.	Bonus Pts.	Point Standing	Behind Leader	Points Leader*
63	1	Feb 19	Daytona — Daytona 500	4	22	200	199	61	Running	$67,915	102	5	22	-83	Marlin
64	2	Feb 26	Rockingham — Goodwrench 500	1	1	492	492	329	Running	167,600	185	10	7	-58	Earnhardt
65	3	Mar 5	Richmond — Pontiac Excitement 400	1	36	400	183	1	DNF— Fuel Pump	28,750	60	5	13	-173	Earnhardt
66	4	Mar 12	Atlanta — Purolator 500	3	1	328	328	250	Running	104,950	185	10	6	-153	Earnhardt
67	5	Mar 26	Darlington — TranSouth Financial 400	1	32	293	200	156	DNF— Crash	20,875	77	10	8	-251	Earnhardt
68	6	Apr 2	Bristol — Food City 500	2	1	500	500	205	Running	67,645	185	10	4	-156	Earnhardt
69	7	Apr 9	North Wilkesboro — First Union 400	1	2	400	400	95	Running	61,625	175	5	3	-164	Earnhardt
70	8	Apr 23	Martinsville — Hanes 500	12	3	356	356	9	Running	36,395	170	5	3	-70	Earnhardt
71	9	Apr 30	Talladega — Winston Select 500	6	2	188	188	12	Running	165,315	175	5	1 (tie)	—	(Earnhardt)[1]
72	10	May 7	Sears Point — Save Mart Supermarkets 300	5	3	74	74	0	Running	41,625	165	0	3	-15	Earnhardt
73	11	May 28	Charlotte — Coca-Cola 600	1	33	400	283	37	DNF— Suspension	64,950	69	5	4	-101	Earnhardt
74	12	Jun 4	Dover — Miller Genuine Draft 500	1	6	500	499	132	Running	37,890	155	5	3	-106	Earnhardt
75	13	Jun 11	Pocono — UAW-GM Teamwork 500	5	16	200	200	124	Running	38,655	125	10	3	-123	Earnhardt
76	14	Jun 18	Michigan — Miller Genuine Draft 400	1	2	200	200	80	Running	72,530	180	10	3	-12	Marlin
77	15	Jul 1	Daytona — Pepsi 400	3	1	160	160	72	Running	96,580	185	10	2	-7	Marlin
78	16	Jul 9	New Hampshire — Slick 50 300	21	1	300	300	126	Running	160,300	185	10	1	+40	(Marlin)
79	17	Jul 16	Pocono — Miller Genuine Draft 500	11	2	200	200	18	Running	48,520	175	5	1	+106	(Marlin)
80	18	Jul 23	Talladega — DieHard 500	3	8	188	188	97	Running	42,375	152	10	1	+78	(Marlin)
81	19	Aug 5	Indianapolis — Brickyard 400	1	6	160	160	35	Running	299,200	155	5	1	+82	(Marlin)
82	20	Aug 13	Watkins Glen — The Bud at the Glen	5	3	90	90	4	Running	42,205	170	5	1	+152	(Marlin)
83	21	Aug 20	Michigan — GM Goodwrench Dealer 400	21	3	200	200	68	Running	46,420	175	10	1	+167	(Marlin)
84	22	Aug 26	Bristol — Goody's 500	4	6	500	500	76	Running	27,865	155	5	1	+176	(Marlin)
85	23	Sept 3	Darlington — Mountain Dew Southern 500	5	1	367	367	54	Running	70,630	180	5	1	+215	(Marlin)
86	24	Sept 9	Richmond — Miller Genuine Draft 400	2	6	400	400	63	Running	38,255	155	5	1	+279	(Earnhardt)
87	25	Sept 17	Dover — MBNA 500	2	1	500	500	400	Running	74,655	185	10	1	+309	(Earnhardt)
88	26	Sept 24	Martinsville — Goody's 500	1	7	500	500	3	Running	25,150	151	5	1	+275	(Earnhardt)
89	27	Oct 1	North Wilkesboro — Tyson/Holly Farms 400	14	3	400	400	12	Running	33,065	170	5	1	+302	(Earnhardt)
90	28	Oct 8	Charlotte — UAW-GM Quality 500	3	30	334	321	23	Running	25,915	78	5	1	+205	(Earnhardt)
91	29	Oct 22	Rockingham — AC Delco 400	4	20	393	391	57	Running	25,550	108	5	1	+162	(Earnhardt)
92	30	Oct 29	Phoenix — Dura-Lube 500	3	5	312	312	0	Running	33,580	155	0	1	+147	(Earnhardt)
93	31	Nov 12	Atlanta — NAPA 500	8	32	328	314	1	Running	19,975	72	5	1	+34	(Earnhardt)

* — Second-place driver listed in parentheses if Gordon is current points leader.

1—Despite points tie, Gordon assumed points lead due to greater number of victories (3–1).

Most Races Led in a Season
Modern Era

Driver	Races Led	Year
Bobby Allison	30	1972
Bobby Labonte	30	1999
Richard Petty	30	1972
Jeff Gordon	29	1995

Gordon tries to recover his Monte Carlo after a tap from Greg Sack (No. 32) on lap 155 during the 1995 AC Delco 500 at Rockingham. Gordon was trying to enter pit road when the incident occurred. He eventually fell two laps down and finished 20th. Despite the bad luck, he won his first Winston Cup championship three weeks later in Atlanta.

"When Jeff goes on the *Letterman* show, he takes all of us with him. His success has been great for NASCAR and every one of us."
—Kyle Petty, *Time*

No driver took advantage of the 1995 re-introduction of the Monte Carlo to Winston Cup racing quite like Jeff Gordon. He won seven times and led a career-high 2,600 laps while winning the 1995 NASCAR championship.

1996: Consistency Trumps Victories

Jeff Gordon fans, perhaps even the driver himself, spent the winter of 1996 cursing the Winston Cup series' point system. Designed to reward consistency, the point system played into the hands of teammate Terry Labonte and left Gordon out in the cold.

Gordon finished with an impressive 10 wins in 1996 but lost the championship to the steady Labonte (who had just two wins) by 37 points. The seemingly incongruous result reopened a debate that had flared up most notably in 1993 when Rusty Wallace (10 wins) out-won Dale Earnhardt (six) but finished a distant second in the points race.

Ultimately, however, Gordon's downfall was of his own making. As he had demonstrated in his previous three seasons, the young driver tended to finish well (indeed, very well). Or he finished very poorly. In his first 92 races, Gordon tallied 48 Top 10s and 23 finishes of 28th or worse.

In 1996, the propensity to finish deep in the field cost him the championship. Gordon and Labonte each ended the season with 24 Top 10s and 7 finishes of 11th or worse. A comparison of their average finish and point totals in Top 10 finishes versus the other seven races in which they finished outside of the Top 10 reveals Labonte's advantage (see chart):

Driver	Avg. Fin. in Top 10	Top 10 Fin. Points	Avg. Fin. Outside of Top 10	Other Fin. Points	Total Points
Jeff Gordon	2.7	4,136	32.7	484	4,620
Terry Labonte	3.6	3,988	24.1	669	4,657

As illustrated, Gordon's bad days had a much greater negative effect than Labonte's. The low point of the 1996 season came immediately for Gordon. Early exits from the season-opening Daytona 500 (in which he finished 42nd) and the following weekend at Rockingham (40th) pushed Gordon back to an all-time career-low 43rd position in the point standings.

Gordon's response to his slow start was admirable, however. He won three of the next four races and quickly climbed to second in the standings. Later, he nearly won five straight races during a streak in which he won a second straight Southern 500 at Darlington, finished second at Richmond (by .1 seconds to Ernie Irvan), and won at Dover, Martinsville and North Wilkesboro.

That incredible streak gave Gordon a 111-point lead over Labonte with just four races remaining. All the hard work washed away, however, when Gordon surrendered his lead the following weekend at Charlotte. Labonte won while Gordon finished 31st, allowing Labonte to pull within a point in the point standings. Gordon ceded the lead for good the next week at Rockingham.

Gordon in 1996

Category	Total	Rank	1996 Leader*
Money	$3,428,485	2nd	Terry Labonte—4,030,648
Total Points	4,620	2nd	Terry Labonte—4,657
Avg. Start	6.3	1st	(Mark Martin—8.8)
Avg. Finish	9.5	3rd	Terry Labonte—8.2
Wins	10	1st	(Rusty Wallace—5)
Top 5s	21	T-1st	(Terry Labonte—21)
Top 10s	24	T-1st	(Terry Labonte—24)
DNFs	5	18th	Andretti, Cope, D. Waltrip—11
Poles	5	1st	(B. & T. Labonte, Martin—4)
Front Row Starts	15	1st	(Mark Martin—6)
Laps Led	2,314	1st	(Terry Labonte—973)
Races Led	25	1st	(Terry Labonte—22)
Times Led	97	1st	(Terry Labonte—58)
Miles Led	2,386	1st	(Terry Labonte—1,214)
Times Led Most Laps	10	1st	(Terry Labonte—4)
Bonus Points	175	1st	(Terry Labonte—130)
Laps Completed	8,972	12th	Dale Earnhardt—9,530
Miles Completed	10,517	19th	Dale Earnhardt—11,523
Points per Race	149.0	2nd	Terry Labonte—150.2
Fin. on Lead Lap	24	T-1st	(Terry Labonte—24)

* Second-place driver or co-leader listed in parentheses if Gordon is category leader.

1996 Performance Chart
No. 24 Hendrick Motorsports Chevrolet

Career Race	Race No.	Date	Race	St.	Fin.	Total Laps	Laps Completed	Laps Led	Condition	Money	Pts.	Bonus Pts.	Point Standing	Behind Leader	Points Leader*
94	1	Feb 18	Daytona — Daytona 500	8	42	200	13	0	DNF— Handling	$59,052	37	0	42	-143	Jarrett
95	2	Feb 25	Rockingham — Goodwrench Service 400	2	40	393	134	0	DNF— Engine	31,730	43	0	43	-275	Jarrett
96	3	Mar 3	Richmond — Pontiac Excitement 400	2	1	400	400	124	Running	92,400	180	10	27	-270	Jarrett
97	4	Mar 10	Atlanta — Purolator 500	21	3	328	328	24	Running	61,600	170	5	16	-230	Jarrett
98	5	Mar 24	Darlington — TranSouth Financial 400	2	1	293	293	189	Running	97,310	185	10	9	-168	Jarrett
99	6	Mar 31	Bristol — Food City 500	8	1	342	342	148	Running	83,765	185	10	6	-133	Jarrett
100	7	Apr 14	North Wilkesboro — First Union 400	17	2	400	400	0	Running	52,750	170	0	5	-97	Jarrett
101	8	Apr 21	Martinsville — Goody's Headache Powder 500	13	3	500	500	211	Running	57,495	175	10	2	-76	Earnhardt
102	9	Apr 28	Talladega — Winston Select 500	11	33	188	141	18	DNF — Crash	34,325	69	5	4	-177	Earnhardt
103	10	May 5	Sears Point — Save Mart Supermarkets 300	6	6	74	74	12	Running	48,145	155	5	4	-187	Earnhardt
104	11	May 26	Charlotte — Coca-Cola 600	1	4	400	400	101	Running	118,200	165	5	4	-197	Earnhardt
105	12	Jun 2	Dover — Miller 500	1	1	500	500	307	Running	138,730	185	10	3	-182	Earnhardt
106	13	Jun 16	Pocono — UAW-GM Teamwork 500	1	1	200	200	94	Running	96,980	185	10	3	-64	Earnhardt
107	14	Jun 23	Michigan — Miller 400	7	6	200	200	40	Running	41,650	155	5	3	-47	Earnhardt
108	15	Jul 6	Daytona — Pepsi 400	1	3	117	117	9	Running	63,735	170	5	3	-37	Earnhardt
109	16	Jul 14	New Hampshire — Jiffy Lube 300	16	34	300	253	59	DNF— Ignition	35,875	71	10	3	-116	T. Labonte
110	17	Jul 21	Pocono — Miller 500	15	7	200	200	1	Running	35,825	151	5	3	-80	T. Labonte
111	18	Jul 28	Talladega — DieHard 500	2	1	129	129	37	Running	272,550	180	5	1	+9	(T. Labonte)
112	19	Aug 3	Indianapolis — Brickyard 400	1	37	160	40	3	DNF— Crash	137,591	57	5	4	-104	T. Labonte
113	20	Aug 11	Watkins Glen — The Bud at the Glen	5	4	90	90	0	Running	44,370	160	0	3	-119	T. Labonte
114	21	Aug 18	Michigan — GM Goodwrench Dealer 400	7	5	200	200	0	Running	44,040	155	0	2	-134	T. Labonte
115	22	Aug 24	Bristol — Goody's Headache Powder 500	2	2	500	500	99	Running	54,590	175	5	2	-114	T. Labonte
116	23	Sept 1	Darlington — Mountain Dew Southern 500	2	1	367	367	52	Running	99,630	180	5	2	-24	T. Labonte
117	24	Sept 7	Richmond — Miller 400	2	2	400	400	168	Running	59,640	180	10	2	-4	T. Labonte
118	25	Sept 15	Dover — MBNA 500	3	1	500	500	203	Running	153,630	185	10	1	+76	(T. Labonte)
119	26	Sept 22	Martinsville — Hanes 500	10	1	500	500	134	Running	93,825	180	5	1	+81	(T. Labonte)
120	27	Sept 29	North Wilkesboro — Tyson Holly Farms 400	2	1	400	400	207	Running	91,350	185	10	1	+111	(T. Labonte)
121	28	Oct 6	Charlotte — UAW-GM Quality 500	2	31	334	319	14	Running	35,070	75	5	1	+1	(T. Labonte)
122	29	Oct 20	Rockingham — AC Delco 400	3	12	393	392	1	Running	35,000	132	5	2	-32	T. Labonte
123	30	Oct 27	Phoenix — Dura-Lube 500	19	5	312	312	0	Running	45,065	155	0	2	-47	T. Labonte
124	31	Nov 10	Atlanta — NAPA 500	2	3	328	328	59	Running	71,600	170	5	2	-37	T. Labonte

* — Second-place driver listed in parentheses if Gordon is current points leader

1997: Second Championship, Last Winston Million

The statistics are overwhelming, but one aspect of the 1997 season best illustrates Jeff Gordon's success: the booing and jeering from the stands became thunderous, exceeded in volume only by the cheers that greeted his every (though relatively rare) misfortune.

Gordon's fifth season on the Winston Cup circuit was magical—and maddening for the ever-growing anti-Gordon legions who grew tired of his unceasing success. In addition to winning a second championship and becoming the first driver to reach $6 million in winnings (leapfrogging the $5 million plateau), Gordon nabbed another 10 victories, won the Daytona 500 for the first time, claimed a record third-straight Southern 500, and, perhaps most impressively, became just the second driver ever to win the Winston Million.

In its 13th and final season the Winston Million, a $1 million bonus posted by R. J. Reynolds, the Winston Cup series sponsor, was offered to any driver who could win three of the four biggest events on the schedule. These were the Daytona 500, the Winston 500 at Talladega, the Coca-Cola 600 at Charlotte, and the Southern 500 at Darlington. Only Bill Elliott had met the challenge in 1985, the Winston Million's inaugural season.

Gordon replicated Elliott's feat by taking the Daytona 500, winning the rain-shortened 600, and by outlasting Jeff Burton in a memorable late-race Southern 500 showdown.

Equally impressive for Gordon was the sheer breadth of his talent. His wins came on new tracks (California), old tracks (Darlington), short tracks (Bristol, Martinsville), big tracks (Daytona, Charlotte), high-banked tracks (Rockingham), flat tracks (New Hampshire), and, for the first time, a road course (Watkins Glen).

Gordon's mastery extended to the series' nonpoints races. He won the season-opening Busch Clash (an exhibition race pitting the previous season's pole winners) and left the field in the Winston all-start race. In 1997, just about any challenge the Winston Cup schedule presented, Gordon and his DuPont team were equal to the task.

The only weakness detectable in Gordon was his inability to close the door on the championship. As in 1995 (which he survived) and in 1996 (which he didn't), Gordon allowed a comfortable lead to fade in the final weeks of the season. With two races remaining, he held a 125-point lead. But a 17th-place in Phoenix and a nearly disastrous closing weekend at Atlanta—where Gordon came from the back of the field and finished 17th—allowed Dale Jarrett to close to within 14 points of Gordon in the final standings. Rather than winning the championship going away, Gordon won the title by the fourth smallest margin in Winston Cup history.

Gordon in 1997

Category	Total	Rank	1997 Leader*
Money	$6,375,658	1st	(Dale Jarrett—3,240,542)
Total Points	4,710	1st	(Dale Jarrett—4,696)
Avg. Start	9.4	2nd	Dale Jarrett—7.2
Avg. Finish	9.6	2nd	Mark Martin—8.9
Wins	10	1st	(Dale Jarrett—7)
Top 5s	22	1st	(Dale Jarrett—20)
Top 10s	23	2nd	Mark Martin—24
DNFs	2	40th	Dallenbach, K & R Wallace —10
Poles	1	11th	B. Labonte, Jarrett, Martin — 3
Front Row Starts	6	T-1st	D. Jarrett, M. Martin—6
Laps Led	1,647	2nd	Dale Jarrett—2,083
Races Led	24	1st	(Dale Jarrett—22)
Times Led	63	2nd	Dale Jarrett—71
Miles Led	1,838	2nd	Dale Jarrett—2,541
Times Led Most Laps	4	2nd	Dale Jarrett—8
Bonus Points	140	2nd	Dale Jarrett—150
Laps Completed	9,276	14th	Dale Jarrett—9,769
Miles Completed	11,989	14th	Dale Jarrett—12,652
Points per Race	147.2	1st	(Dale Jarrett—146.8)
Fin. on Lead Lap	22	4th	Jeff Burton—24

* Second-place driver or co-leader listed in parentheses if Gordon is category leader.

1997 Performance Chart
No. 24 Hendrick Motorsports Chevrolet

Career Race	Race No.	Date	Race	St.	Fin.	Total Laps	Laps Completed	Laps Led	Condition	Money	Pts.	Bonus Pts.	Point Standing	Behind Leader	Points Leader*
125	1	Feb 16	Daytona — Daytona 500	6	1	200	200	40	Running	$456,999	180	5	1	+10	(T. Labonte)
126	2	Feb 23	Rockingham — Goodwrench Service 400	4	1	393	393	43	Running	93,115	180	5	1	+40	(Craven)
127	3	Mar 2	Richmond — Pontiac Excitement 400	2	4	400	399	65	Running	46,200	165	5	1	+63	(T. Labonte)
128	4	Mar 9	Atlanta — Primestar 500	23	42	328	59	0	DNF—Engine	34,770	37	0	4	-72	Jarrett
129	5	Mar 23	Darlington — TranSouth Financial 400	10	3	293	293	16	Running	56,240	170	5	2	-87	Jarrett
130	6	Apr 6	Texas — Interstate Batteries 500	2	30	334	247	69	Running	60,200	78	5	5	-184	Jarrett
131	7	Apr 13	Bristol — Food City 500	5	1	500	500	125	Running	83,640	180	5	3	-164	Jarrett
132	8	Apr 20	Martinsville — Goody's Headache Powder 500	4	1	500	500	431	Running	99,225	185	10	3	-94	Jarrett
133	9	May 4	Sears Point — SaveMart Supermarkets 300	3	2	74	74	0	Running	66,065	170	0	3	-89	Jarrett
134	10	May 10	Talladega — Winston 500	11	5	188	188	13	Running	54,440	160	5	2	-39	T. Labonte
135	11	May 25	Charlotte — Coca-Cola 600	1	1	333	333	44	Running	224,900	180	5	2	-6	T. Labonte
136	12	Jun 1	Dover — Miller 500	2	26	500	490	18	Running	33,470	90	5	2	-37	T. Labonte
137	13	Jun 8	Pocono — Pocono 500	11	1	200	200	59	Running	166,080	180	5	1	0	(T. Labonte)[1]
138	14	Jun 15	Michigan — Miller 400	12	5	200	200	0	Running	47,425	155	0	1	+46	(Martin)
139	15	Jun 22	California — California 500	3	1	250	250	113	Running	144,600	185	10	1	+92	(Martin)
140	16	Jul 5	Daytona — Pepsi 400	4	21	160	160	1	Running	85,135	105	5	1	+54	(T. Labonte)
141	17	Jul 13	New Hampshire — Jiffy Lube 300	29	23	300	298	0	Running	37,975	94	0	2	-3	T. Labonte
142	18	Jul 20	Pocono — Pennsylvania 500	6	2	200	200	53	Running	56,745	175	5	1	+64	(Martin)
143	19	Aug 2	Indianapolis — Brickyard 400	24	4	160	160	25	Running	223,675	165	5	1	+79	(Martin)
144	20	Aug 10	Watkins Glen — Bud at the Glen	11	1	90	90	32	Running	139,120	185	10	1	+109	(Martin)
145	21	Aug 17	Michigan — DeVilbiss 400	17	2	200	200	1	Running	85,728	175	5	1	+99	(Martin)
146	22	Aug 23	Bristol — Goody's Headache Powder 500	2	35	500	365	188	DNF— Crash	33,955	63	5	2	-13	Martin
147	23	Aug 31	Darlington — Mountain Dew Southern 500	7	1	367	367	116	Running	1,131,330	180	5	1	+25	(Martin)
148	24	Sept 6	Richmond — Exide 400	10	3	400	400	0	Running	52,355	165	0	1	+97	(Martin)
149	25	Sept 14	New Hampshire — CMT 300	13	1	300	300	137	Running	188,625	185	10	1	+139	(Martin)
150	26	Sept 21	Dover — MBNA 400	2	7	400	398	11	Running	38,190	151	5	1	+105	(Martin)
151	27	Sept 29	Martinsville — Hanes 500	11	4	500	500	21	Running	40,225	165	5	1	+135	(Martin)
152	28	Oct 5	Charlotte — UAW-GM Quality 500	4	5	334	334	0	Running	62,200	155	0	1	+125	(Martin)
153	29	Oct 12	Talladega — DieHard 500	8	35	188	153	3	Running	38,915	63	5	1	+110	(Martin)
154	30	Oct 27	Rockingham — AC Delco 400	5	4	393	393	23	Running	41,150	165	5	1	+125	(Martin)
155	31	Nov 2	Phoenix — Dura-Lube 500	12	17	312	310	0	Running	29,880	112	0	1	+77	(Jarrett)
156	32	Nov 16	Atlanta — NAPA 500	37	17	325	322	0	Running	41,155	112	0	1	+14	(Jarrett)

* — Second-place driver listed in parentheses if Gordon is current points leader

[1] — Despite points tie, Gordon listed as leader due to more wins (6 - 0)

In 1997, Jeff Gordon achieved a career milestone by winning his first Daytona 500. He piloted the No. 24 car to a Hendrick Motorsports sweep of the top three positions in the race. Then-teammate Ricky Craven (No. 25) finished third, while Terry Labonte finished second.

In 1997, Jeff Gordon started the season with consecutive victories at Daytona and Rockingham. Here, he tries to put a lap on Kenny Wallace (No. 55 Square-D) and Chad Little (No. 97 John Deere). In his career on the 1.017-mile oval, Gordon has led 765, or 11.3 percent, of the laps he has run at the track.

"[He] has something extra, like Michael Jordan and Mickey Mantle had. He has a different sense of time than you and I. He can slow the race down in his mind, see things coming around and react before the next guy."
—Ray Evernham, Gordon's former crew chief, *Time*

1998: Third Championship, A Season for the Ages

Just when it appeared Jeff Gordon couldn't possibly improve on his performance, he reached historic marks and joined elite company in 1998. Among his accomplishments, Gordon

· won his third Winston Cup championship, tying with Lee Petty, David Pearson, Cale Yarborough, and Darrell Waltrip (Only Dale Earnhardt and Richard Petty (seven titles each) have won more.)

· tied Richard Petty for most wins in a season (13) in the modern era

· won four straight races, tying the modern era record set by Cale Yarborough in 1976 and matched by Darrell Waltrip (1981), Dale Earnhardt (1987), Harry Gant (1991), Bill Elliott (1992), and Mark Martin (1993)

· became the first driver to reach $9 million in earnings, breaking his own record and leapfrogging the $7 and $8 million plateaus

· amassed the most points ever (5,328) under the current point system (Gordon became the first driver to amass 5,000 championship points under the current system since Yarborough's 5,000 in 1977.)

· collected the most Top 5 finishes (26) in a single season in the modern era

· set the modern era record for most lead-lap finishes (28)

· finished 17 consecutive races in the Top 5, setting the modern-era record and nearly matching the all-time NASCAR record set by David Pearson in 1968

· posted the fourth-best average finish in the modern era

· finished with the third-best average points per race (161.5) since the current point system was instituted in 1975, behind only Cale Yarborough (166.7 in 1977) and Dale Earnhardt (162.1 in 1987)

· a year after winning the last Winston Million bonus offered, became the first driver to win a No Bull 5 Million bonus at the Brickyard 400 (Gordon then became the first driver to win more than one No Bull 5 race when he won the Southern 500.)

· bettering his own record, became the first driver ever to win four straight Southern 500s

If the list above doesn't go far enough in illustrating Gordon's dominance in 1998, consider the following: In the season's final 19 race, Gordon finished in first or second place 15 times. During one midseason stretch (starting with Sears Point in June and ending with Darlington's Southern 500 in September), Gordon won seven of nine races; he finished third and fifth in the other two.

Even more important for Gordon was his strong finish. In the previous three seasons, Gordon allowed strong leads to evaporate. In 1998, he won three of the final four races of the year and swelled his lead over Mark Martin to 364, the sixth-largest winning margin under the current point system.

Gordon in 1998

Category	Total	Rank	1998 Leader (2nd Place)
Money	$9,306,584	1st	(Mark Martin—4,309,006)
Total Points	5,328	1st	(Mark Martin—4,964)
Avg. Start	6.9	1st	(Dale Jarrett—8.7)
Avg. Finish	5.7	1st	(Mark Martin—8.6)
Wins	13	1st	(Mark Martin—7)
Top 5s	26	1st	(Mark Martin—22)
Top 10s	28	1st	(Mark Martin—26)
DNFs	2	40th	Kenny Wallace—13
Poles	7	1st	(Rusty Wallace—4)
Front Row Starts	11	1st	(Rusty Wallace—7)
Laps Led	1,717	2nd	Mark Martin—1,730
Races Led	26	1st	(Mark Martin—23)
Times Led	76	1st	(Mark Martin—74)
Miles Led	2,765	1st	(Mark Martin—2,171)
Times Led Most Laps	8	T-1st	(Mark Martin—8)
Bonus Points	170	1st	(Mark Martin—155)
Laps Completed	9,818	3rd	Bobby Hamilton—9,840
Miles Completed	12,785	1st	(Bobby Hamilton—12,760)
Points per Race	161.5	1st	(Mark Martin—150.4)
Fin. on Lead Lap	28	1st	(Mark Martin—26)

*Second-place driver or co-leader listed in parentheses if Gordon is category leader.

1998 Performance Chart
No. 24 Hendrick Motorsports Chevrolet

Career Race	Race No.	Date	Race	St.	Fin.	Total Laps	Laps Completed	Laps Led	Condition	Money	Pts.	Bonus Pts.	Point Standing	Behind Leader	Points Leader*
157	1	Feb 15	Daytona — Daytona 500	29	16	200	200	56	Running	$114,730	120	5	15	-65	Earnhardt
158	2	Feb 22	Rockingham — GM Goodwrench Service Plus 400	4	1	393	393	73	Running	90,090	180	5	3	-35	R. Wallace
159	3	Mar 1	Las Vegas — Las Vegas 400	5	17	267	266	0	Running	76,200	112	0	6	-93	R. Wallace
160	4	Mar 9	Atlanta — Primestar 500	9	19	325	323	0	Running	44,865	106	0	7	-147	R. Wallace
161	5	Mar 22	Darlington — TranSouth Financial 400	24	2	293	293	0	Running	75,075	170	0	4	-147	R. Wallace
162	6	Mar 29	Bristol — Food City 500	2	1	500	500	63	Running	90,860	180	5	3	-41	R. Wallace
163	7	Apr 5	Texas — Texas 500	17	31	334	252	0	DNF— Handling	66,900	70	0	5	-98	R. Wallace
164	8	Apr 20	Martinsville — Goody's Headache Powder 500	3	8	500	499	19	Running	47,000	147	5	4	-106	R. Wallace
165	9	Apr 26	Talladega — Diehard 500	6	5	188	188	3	Running	74,490	160	5	5	-73	R. Wallace
166	10	May 3	California — California 500	1	4	250	250	23	Running	98,800	165	5	3	-47	Mayfield
167	11	May 24	Charlotte — Coca-Cola 600	1	1	400	400	53	Running	429,950	180	5	1	+27	(Mayfield)
168	12	May 31	Dover — MBNA Platinum 400	2	3	400	400	375	Running	79,350	175	10	1	+47	(Mayfield)
169	13	Jun 6	Richmond — Pontiac Excitement 400	1	37	400	372	2	DNF— Crash	44,975	57	5	3	-46	Mayfield
170	14	Jun 14	Michigan — Miller Lite 400	4	3	200	200	132	Running	84,375	175	10	2	-26	Mayfield
171	15	Jun 21	Pocono — Pocono 500	1	2	200	200	17	Running	79,500	175	5	2	-36	Mayfield
172	16	Jun 28	Sears Point — Save Mart/Kragen 350	1	1	112	112	48	Running	160,675	185	10	1	+40	(Mayfield)
173	17	Jul 12	New Hampshire — Jiffy Lube 300	2	3	300	300	73	Running	116,025	170	5	1	+52	(Martin)
174	18	Jul 26	Pocono — Pennsylvania 500	2	1	200	200	164	Running	165,495	185	10	1	+62	(Martin)
175	19	Aug 1	Indianapolis — Brickyard 400	3	1	160	160	97	Running	1,637,625	185	10	1	+72	(Martin)
176	20	Aug 9	Watkins Glen — The Bud at the Glen	1	1	90	90	55	Running	152,970	185	10	1	+82	(Martin)
177	21	Aug 16	Michigan — Pepsi 400	3	1	200	200	9	Running	120,302	180	5	1	+97	(Martin)
178	22	Aug 22	Bristol — Goody's Headache Powder 500	7	5	500	500	0	Running	58,650	155	0	1	+67	(Martin)
179	23	Aug 30	New Hampshire — Farm Aid on CMT 300	1	1	300	300	68	Running	205,400	180	5	1	+67	(Martin)
180	24	Sept 6	Darlington — Mountain Dew Southern 500	5	1	367	367	64	Running	1,134,655	180	5	1	+199	(Martin)
181	25	Sept 12	Richmond — Exide Batteries 400	5	2	400	400	30	Running	85,190	175	5	1	+204	(Martin)
182	26	Sept 20	Dover — MBNA Gold 400	6	2	400	400	6	Running	77,005	175	5	1	+194	(Martin)
183	27	Sept 27	Martinsville — NAPA Autocare 500	3	2	500	500	0	Running	73,525	170	0	1	+199	(Martin)
184	28	Oct 4	Charlotte — UAW-GM Quality 500	26	5	334	334	47	Running	79,450	160	5	1	+174	(Martin)
185	29	Oct 11	Talladega — Winston 500	6	2	188	188	49	Running	86,245	175	5	1	+288	(Martin)
186	30	Oct 17	Daytona — Pepsi 400	8	1	160	160	49	Running	184,325	185	10	1	+358	(Martin)
187	31	Oct 25	Phoenix — Dura Lube/KMart 500	12	7	257	257	0	Running	47,040	146	0	1	+329	(Martin)
188	32	Nov 1	Rockingham — AC Delco 400	9	1	393	393	29	Running	111,575	180	5	1	+343	(Martin)
189	33	Nov 8	Atlanta — NAPA 500	21	1	221	221	113	Running	164,450	185	10	1	+364	(Martin)

* — Second-place driver listed in parentheses if Gordon is current points leader

"Jeff is one of those guys who comes along every 25 years or so, like a Foyt or a Petty or an Andretti."

—Humpy Wheeler, Charlotte Motor Speedway president, *Stock Car Racing*

Gordon hoists the winner's trophy at Michigan in 1998, a significant victory for two reasons. First, it marked Gordon's first and only win on the track. Second, with his victory, Gordon tied the Modern Era NASCAR record of four consecutive wins set by Cale Yarborough and later matched by Darrell Waltrip, Bill Elliott, Dale Earnhardt, Harry Gant, and Mark Martin. Gordon had won the three previous races at Pocono, Indianapolis, and Watkins Glen.

In 1998, Jeff Gordon was the center of the Winston Cup universe. He won a modern-era tying 13 races and led the series in wins, money, average start, average finish, Top 5s, Top 10s, poles, front row starts, and races led. He won an all-time single-season record $9.3 million and took the Winston Cup title by 364 points.

"A lot of people will tell you Gordon was made because he came into Winston Cup and got with Hendricks, a big-money team with good equipment. But, you know, it was pretty much the other way around. Gordon kind of made that team."
—Sterling Marlin, *Philadelphia Inquirer*

1999: Implosion

If all good things must come to an end, apparently great things tend to implode. For Jeff Gordon, a great run ended chaotically. After a magical four-year stretch, during which Gordon won three championships, 40 races, and $23.5 million, the world crashed around the No. 24 Hendrick Motorsports team. Gordon's crew chief, Ray Evernham, left to lead Dodge's return to Winston Cup racing. He watched his hyper-efficient crew, the Rainbow Warriors, defect to Dale Jarrett's team, and he fell victim to racing luck frequently while slipping to sixth place in the final point standings (a ghastly 642 points behind champion Jarrett).

The omen was Gordon's crash at Texas in the season's sixth race. On lap 69, Gordon cut his right front tire, sending his Chevy hurtling into the wall coming off of Turn 4. The exit relegated Gordon to 43rd-place in the finishing order, the first and only time in his career that he has finished so low. Until the Texas accident, Gordon looked strong. He won his second Daytona 500, and a then-American racing record $2,174,246 purse. Another win at Atlanta and thirds at Las Vegas and Darlington put Gordon in second place in the point standings, just seven points behind Jeff Burton.

Texas, however, augured bad times. Crashes and mechanical problems, which Gordon had mostly avoided for four years, stung him six more times in 1999. The worst luck, of course, was the spectacular season assembled by Jarrett. Even when Gordon finished strongly, he lost or gained little ground on Jarrett. By the fall Dover race, Gordon was trailing Jarrett by 423 points. At Dover, the worst-kept secret in NASCAR became a reality: The talented tandem of Gordon and Evernham was breaking up. At the fall Dover race, Evernham was present but stood back as Brian Whitesell assumed crew chief responsibilities.

Gordon finished 17th that Sunday, but his immediate reaction to Evernham's departure was impressive. He and Whitesell won their first two races together at Martinsville and Charlotte. Thereafter, however, the results were mixed. Gordon led the most laps at the October Talladega race, but got shuffled back to 12th at the end. At Phoenix, he came up with his best qualifying effort at the track—second—but quickly faded, eventually finishing 10th. The inaugural Homestead race pointed out his and other Chevy teams' problems on flat tracks (Gordon started and finished 10th). Atlanta was, well, a disaster.

In the end, the huge changes in Gordon's racing life—crew chief left, crew left, good luck left—overshadowed a pretty solid season. Gordon finished with seven wins (leading the series for a record fifth consecutive season), won a series-leading seven poles, and led the most laps.

Gordon in 1999

Category	Total	Rank	1999 Leader
Money	$5,858,633	2nd	Dale Jarrett—6,649,596
Total Points	4,620	6th	Dale Jarrett—5,262
Avg. Start	7.4	1st	(Mark Martin—8.2)
Avg. Finish	12.9	7th	Dale Jarrett—6.8
Wins	7	1st	(Jeff Burton—6)
Top 5s	18	4th	Dale Jarrett—24
Top 10s	21	5th	Dale Jarrett—29
DNFs	7	4th	Andretti, Craven, M. Waltrip—10
Poles	7	1st	(Bobby Labonte—5)
Front Row Starts	9	1st	(B. Labonte, R. Wallace—9)
Laps Led	1,319	1st	(Tony Stewart—1,227)
Races Led	26	2nd	Bobby Labonte—30
Times Led	86	1st	(Bobby Labonte—81)
Miles Led	1,923	1st	(Dale Jarrett—1,812)
Times Led Most Laps	6	T-1st	(Jeff Burton—6)
Bonus Points	160	2nd	Bobby Labonte—165
Laps Completed	9,384	26th	Bobby Labonte—10,013
Miles Completed	12,132	26th	Bobby Labonte—13,135
Points per Race	135.9	6th	Dale Jarrett—154.8
Fin. on Lead Lap	23	5th	D. Jarrett, B. Labonte—28

* Second-place driver or co-leader listed in parentheses if Gordon is category leader.

"I thought about just holding [Gordon] down on the apron and driving him right into the back of [Ricky] Rudd's car. I thought Gordon would maybe get out of the throttle a little bit, but he wouldn't. He was going. To do it over again, I probably would have held him down there and waited for the outcome."
—Rusty Wallace, on Gordon's daring late-race pass on Wallace during the 1999 Daytona 500 (which Gordon won), *Sports Illustrated*

1999 Performance Chart
No. 24 Hendrick Motorsports Chevrolet

Career Race	Race No.	Date	Race	St.	Fin.	Total Laps	Laps Completed	Laps Led	Condition	Money	Pts.	Bonus Pts.	Point Standing	Behind Leader	Points Leader*
190	1	Feb 14	Daytona — Daytona 500	1	1	200	200	17	Running	$2,172,246	180	5	1	+10	(Earnhardt)
191	2	Feb 21	Rockingham — Dura-Lube/Big Kmart 400	3	39	393	310	89	DNF— Engine	44,125	51	5	11	-84	Skinner
192	3	Mar 7	Las Vegas — Las Vegas 400	11	3	267	267	1	Running	179,400	170	5	5	-74	Skinner
193	4	Mar 14	Atlanta — Cracker Barrel Old Country Store 500	8	1	325	325	109	Running	117,650	185	10	3	-44	Skinner
194	5	Mar 21	Darlington — TranSouth Financial 400	1	3	164	164	50	Running	83,940	170	5	2	-7	J. Burton
195	6	Mar 28	Texas — Primestar 500	8	43	334	68	0	DNF— Crash	60,000	34	0	4	-119	J. Burton
196	7	Apr 11	Bristol — Food City 500	2	6	500	500	0	Running	55,970	150	0	5	-124	J. Burton
197	8	Apr 18	Martinsville — Goody's Body Pain 500	9	3	500	500	163	Running	71,800	170	5	4	-129	J. Burton
198	9	Apr 25	Talladega — Diehard 500	13	38	188	112	0	DNF— Handling	55,250	49	0	5	-210	J. Burton
199	10	May 2	California — California 500	5	1	250	250	151	Running	155,890	185	10	4	-200	J. Burton
200	11	May 15	Richmond — Pontiac Excitement 400	1	31	400	388	18	Running	54,275	75	5	5	-250	Jarrett
201	12	May 30	Charlotte — Coca-Cola 600	10	39	400	341	1	DNF— Handling	56,780	51	5	8	-354	Jarrett
202	13	Jun 6	Dover — MBNA Platinum 400	14	2	400	400	104	Running	96,805	175	5	6	-339	Jarrett
203	14	Jun 13	Michigan — Kmart 400	1	2	200	200	20	Running	90,050	175	5	6	-349	Jarrett
204	15	Jun 20	Pocono — Pocono 500	17	2	200	200	10	Running	111,220	175	5	5	-349	Jarrett
205	16	Jun 27	Sears Point — Save Mart/Kragen 350k	1	1	112	112	80	Running	125,040	185	10	5	-314	Jarrett
206	17	Jul 3	Daytona — Pepsi 400	11	21	160	160	0	Running	56,960	100	0	5	-394	Jarrett
207	18	Jul 11	New Hampshire — Jiffy Lube 300	1	3	300	300	54	Running	97,050	170	5	5	-389	Jarrett
208	19	Jul 25	Pocono — Pennsylvania 500	7	32	200	186	22	DNF— Suspension	49,990	72	5	6	-492	Jarrett
209	20	Aug 7	Indianapolis — Brickyard 400	1	3	160	160	24	Running	262,800	170	5	6	-507	Jarrett
210	21	Aug 15	Watkins Glen — Frontier @ the Glen	3	1	90	90	55	Running	119,860	185	10	5	-482	Jarrett
211	22	Aug 22	Michigan — Pepsi 400	9	2	200	200	73	Running	83,030	180	10	4	-467	Jarrett
212	23	Aug 28	Bristol — Goody's Headache Powder 500	4	4	500	500	48	Running	71,505	165	5	4	-351	Jarrett
213	24	Sept 5	Darlington — Pepsi Southern 500	4	13	270	270	41	Running	53,410	129	5	4	-342	Jarrett
214	25	Sept 11	Richmond — Exide Batteries 400	6	40	400	311	56	DNF— Transmission	50,625	48	5	6	-459	Jarrett
215	26	Sept 19	New Hampshire — Dura-Lube/Kmart 300	19	5	300	300	0	Running	88,440	155	5	6	-418	Jarrett
216	27	Sept 26	Dover — MBNA Gold 400	7	17	400	397	14	Running	49,940	117	5	6	-471	Jarrett
217	28	Oct 3	Martinsville — NAPA AutoCare 500	5	1	500	500	29	Running	110,090	180	5	6	-425	Jarrett
218	29	Oct 10	Charlotte — UAW-GM Quality 500	22	1	334	334	16	Running	140,350	180	5	4	-396	Jarrett
219	30	Oct 17	Talladega — Winston 500	14	12	188	188	71	Running	75,675	137	10	4	-434	Jarrett
220	31	Oct 24	Rockingham — Pop Secret Popcorn 400	4	11	393	392	0	Running	50,790	130	0	4	-474	Jarrett
221	32	Nov 7	Phoenix — Checker Auto Parts/Dura-Lube 500K	2	10	312	312	0	Running	78,465	134	0	5	-495	Jarrett
222	33	Nov 14	Homestead — Pennzoil 400	10	10	267	266	3	Running	70,590	139	5	6	-516	Jarrett
223	34	Nov 21	Atlanta — NAPA 500	16	38	325	181	0	DNF— Engine	59,350	49	0	6	-642	Jarrett

* — Second-place driver listed in parentheses if Gordon is current points leader

Ray Evernham's final race as Jeff Gordon's crew chief came 27 races into the 1999 season at Dover. Gordon finished that race in 17th, three laps off the pace. He responded to Evernham's departure by winning the first two races with interim crew chief Brian Whitesell.

Gordon leads the field through pace laps at Indianapolis before the 1999 Brickyard 400, his third Indy pole. Only one other driver (Ernie Irvan) has won more than one pole at Indy. Next to Gordon is Mark Martin (No. 6 Valvoline). In row 2 are David Green (No. 41 Kodiak) and Dale Jarrett (No. 88 Ford Quality Care).

"In quarter-midgets, the other parents would stop and watch him drive. The throttle always made the same sound; it was so smooth. The real fans can tell when he's out there, the rhythm and the ballet he puts on."
—John Bickford, Gordon's step-father, *Orange County Register*

2000: Starting Over

In 2000, for the first time in six years, Jeff Gordon had no impact on a Winston Cup season. Unlike campaigns past, he didn't contend for a championship or win the most races or poles or lead the most laps. Instead, Gordon had another rookie season.

With a new crew chief, a new crew, a new car (the 2000 Monte Carlo), and a new teammate (Jerry Nadeau), Gordon cut nearly every connection he had to his past success. Only his car's paint scheme and his car's owner, Rick Hendrick, remained. The statistics resulting from the massive change in Gordon's racing life were startling. For instance:

· Gordon led none of the 1,000 competitive laps at Martinsville. In his previous 11 starts there, he had led 1,034 laps.
· He was a nonfactor in the 12 races at California, Indianapolis, Pocono, Michigan, Dover, Daytona, and New Hampshire, some of his best racetracks, where he has 18 career wins.
· He led fewer laps in 2000 (425) than he did as a Winston Cup sophomore (446).

The good news for Gordon and his new crew chief, Robbie Loomis, was the steady improvement and strong finish. During the final month of the season, Gordon was the series' best driver, points-wise, even bettering Bobby Labonte, who capped his first championship with a strong finish (see chart).

In fact, following a dismal August (he finished all four August races 23rd or worse), Gordon's team seemed to find its rhythm. He finished 10 of the final 11 races in the Top 9, with the lone disappointing finish caused by a Rusty Wallace–Dale Jarrett crash that consumed Gordon's car at Charlotte. With an impressive average finish of 4.9 in those 10 races, Gordon and crew have their eyes trained on the 2001 title.

Final Month of the 2000 Season Championship Points

Driver	Points
Jeff Gordon	797
Rusty Wallace	736
Bobby Labonte	725
Dale Earnhardt	718
Jeff Burton	683
Steve Park	683

Gordon in 2000

Category	Total	Rank	2000 Leader
Money	$2,703,586	10th	Bobby Labonte—7,041,746
Total Points	4,361	9th	Bobby Labonte—5,130
Avg. Start	12.2	4th	Rusty Wallace—10.0
Avg. Finish	12.9	8th	Bobby Labonte—7.4
Wins	3	5th	Tony Stewart—6
Top 5s	11	9th	Bobby Labonte—19
Top 10s	22	5th	D. Earnhardt, D. Jarrett, B. Labonte—24
DNFs	3	35th	J. Mayfield, S. Pruett—11
Poles	3	3rd	Rusty Wallace—9
Front Row Starts	4	5th	Rusty Wallace—11
Laps Led	425	9th	Rusty Wallace—1,730
Races Led	15	8th	J. Burton, B. Labonte—23
Times Led	41	6th	Rusty Wallace—62
Miles Led	480.9	14th	Rusty Wallace—1,867.8
Times Led Most Laps	2	6th	Rusty Wallace—6
Bonus Points	85	8th	Jeff Burton—140
Laps Completed	9,897	7th	Bobby Labonte—10,158
Miles Completed	12,802.5	7th	Bobby Labonte—13,223.8
Points per Race	128.3	9th	Bobby Labonte—150.9
Fin. on Lead Lap	22	8th	D. Earnhardt, B. Labonte—28

2000 Performance Chart
No. 24 Hendrick Motorsports Chevrolet

Career Race	Race No.	Date	Race	St.	Fin.	Total Laps	Laps Completed	Laps Led	Condition	Money	Pts.	Bonus Pts.	Point Standing	Behind Leader	Points Leader*
224	1	Feb 20	Daytona — Daytona 500	11	34	200	195	0	Running	$106,100	61	0	34	-124	Jarrett
225	2	Feb 27	Rockingham — Dura Lube/Kmart 400	5	10	393	392	16	Running	61,510	139	5	22	-140	Jarrett
226	3	Mar 5	Las Vegas — Carsdirect.com 400	10	28	148	147	0	Running	70,875	79	0	23	-211	B. Labonte
227	4	Mar 12	Atlanta — Cracker Barrel Old Country Store 500	7	9	325	324	4	Running	49,870	143	5	17	-243	B. Labonte
228	5	Mar 19	Darlington — Mall.com 400	1	8	293	293	22	Running	56,915	147	5	13	-225	B. Labonte
229	6	Mar 26	Bristol — Food City 500	3	8	500	500	225	Running	51,295	152	10	10	-223	B. Labonte
230	7	Apr 2	Texas — DirecTV 500	23	25	334	320	0	Running	76,150	88	0	12	-305	B. Labonte
231	8	Apr 9	Martinsville — Goody's Body Pain 500	11	4	500	500	0	Running	65,530	160	0	12	-277	B. Labonte
232	9	Apr 16	Talladega — DieHard 500	36	1	188	188	25	Running	159,755	180	5	7	-221	Martin
233	10	Apr 30	California — NAPA Auto Parts 500	26	11	250	250	0	Running	64,475	130	0	8	-237	B. Labonte
234	11	May 6	Richmond — Pontiac Excitement 400	15	14	400	400	0	Running	46,850	121	0	9	-201	B. Labonte
235	12	May 28	Charlotte — Coca-Cola 600	14	10	400	400	4	Running	78,950	139	5	8	-237	B. Labonte
236	13	Jun 4	Dover — MBNA Platinum 400	19	32	400	380	0	DNF— Crash	63,420	67	0	10	-340	B. Labonte
237	14	Jun 11	Michigan — Kmart 400	3	14	194	193	2	Running	47,250	126	5	10	-384	B. Labonte
238	15	Jun 18	Pocono — Pocono 500	5	8	200	200	0	Running	64,765	142	0	10	-366	B. Labonte
239	16	Jun 25	Sears Point — Save Mart/Kragen 300	5	1	112	112	43	Running	143,025	185	10	10	-341	B. Labonte
240	17	Jul 1	Daytona — Pepsi 400	34	10	160	160	0	Running	74,675	134	0	10	-334	B. Labonte
241	18	Jul 9	New Hampshire – Thatlook.com 300	8	5	273	273	0	Running	74,375	155	0	10	-322	B. Labonte
242	19	Jul 23	Pocono — Pennsylvania 500	5	3	200	200	10	Running	92,045	170	5	8	-307	B. Labonte
243	20	Aug 5	Indianapolis — Brickyard 400	29	33	160	158	0	Running	102,185	64	0	8	-423	B. Labonte
244	21	Aug 13	Watkins Glen — Global Crossing @ The Glen	8	23	90	90	0	Running	46,095	94	0	10	-489	B. Labonte
245	22	Aug 20	Michigan — Pepsi 400	16	36	200	141	0	DNF— Handling	42,205	55	0	10	-604	B. Labonte
246	23	Aug 26	Bristol — Goracing.com 500	2	23	500	499	0	Running	49,985	94	0	10	-633	B. Labonte
247	24	Sept 3	Darlington — Southern 500	10	4	328	328	24	Running	82,540	165	5	10	-648	B. Labonte
248	25	Sept 9	Richmond — Chevrolet Monte Carlo 400[1]	13	1	400	400	15	Running	130,220	80	5	10	-691	B. Labonte
249	26	Sept 17	New Hampshire – Dura Lube 300	18	6	300	300	0	Running	74,575	150	0	10	-711	B. Labonte
250	27	Sept 24	Dover — MBNA.com 400	9	9	400	400	0	Running	70,290	138	0	10	-733	B. Labonte
251	28	Oct 1	Martinsville — NAPA AutoCare 500	5	5	500	500	0	Running	59,075	155	0	9	-712	B. Labonte
252	29	Oct 8	Charlotte — UAW-GM Quality 500	1	39	334	170	1	DNF— Crash	65,980	51	5	10	-841	B. Labonte
253	30	Oct 15	Talladega — Winston 500	8	4	188	188	26	Running	82,100	165	5	9	-808	B. Labonte
254	31	Oct 22	Rockingham — Pop Secret 400	3	2	393	393	4	Running	83,100	175	5	9	-741	B. Labonte
255	32	Nov 5	Phoenix — Checker Auto Parts/DuraLube 500K	24	7	312	312	0	Running	81,550	146	0	9	-755	B. Labonte
256	33	Nov 12	Homestead — Pennzoil 400	28	7	267	266	0	Running	83,725	146	0	9	-774	B. Labonte
257	34	Nov 19	Atlanta — NAPA 500	1	4	325	325	4	Running	88,800	165	5	9	-769	B. Labonte

[1] — Penalized 100 points for illegal intake manifold

"Gordon's a good driver, but he's got a long way to go to win seven or eight championships. Winning one doesn't make him the greatest driver in the world."
—Dale Earnhardt, Winston Cup driver, *USA Today*

Gordon set a Talladega track record in 2000 when he won the DieHard 500 from the 36th starting position, the deepest start for any eventual winner at the 2.66-mile superspeedway. The win snapped a 13-race winless streak.

"We had a three-year agreement with two years in Busch and one in Winston Cup, and he chose not to honor that. We're real hurt. I love him like a son and for him to do this to me is not right."
—Bill Davis, Gordon's Busch Series car owner after Gordon signed a contract to drive in the Winston Cup series with Rick Hendrick, *Atlanta Journal and Constitution*

Fate rained on Jeff Gordon's parade in 2000. Unlike previous seasons, he didn't contend for a championship or win the most races or poles or lead the most laps. Instead, Gordon had another rookie season.

Jeff Gordon's Performance on Current and Former Winston Cup Tracks

The Winston Cup schedule includes a variety of tracks, from short tracks (less than 1 mile, such as Bristol), to 1-mile ovals (Dover) to speedways (less than 2 miles, such as Darlington) to superspeedways (2 miles or greater, such as Talladega) to road courses (Watkins Glen). Each track demands a different touch, a different set of skills. Over the course of a driver's career, patterns emerge that provide a glimpse into the style and skill of a driver. This section lays out in detail Gordon's career on each Winston Cup track.

For each track on which Gordon has competed there is a statistical comparison to determine his place in the track's history. This comparison extends to 22 different statistical categories. Gordon's total for each category is listed, along with his rank and that category's leader. If Gordon is the leader in a category, the second-place driver is listed in parentheses with his total. For the older tracks—that is, tracks that have been part of the Winston Cup circuit for more than 30 years—the comparison is limited to the modern era (1972 to the present).

Accompanying the statistical comparison is a track summary that puts Gordon's career at the track in context or details memorable moments. Perhaps most useful to understanding Gordon's development at each track is the inclusion of a performance chart that lists in detail every race he has run at the track. Listed for each race are the year, date, and race name, along with Gordon's start, finish, total laps, laps completed, laps led, race-ending condition, money, points earned, and bonus points.

Gordon prepares for the final race of 1999 at Atlanta. No track better exemplified Gordon's plight in 1999 than this one. In the track's spring race, he won impressively and seemed on his way to another stellar year. By the time the Winston Cup series returned to Atlanta in November, however, Gordon's team was in disarray, enduring the defections of crew chief Ray Evernham and the majority of the over-the-wall crew that had propelled the team to multiple victories. In a fitting end to a frustrating season, Gordon finished the 1999 Atlanta fall race in 38th place after dropping out early with a blown engine.

Gordon exits his pit with a wave from a crewmember during the 1995 Food City 500. Since 1995, the half-mile track has been one of Gordon's best qualifying tracks. Between 1995 and 2000, he started 12 consecutive races from a Top 8 starting position. *Jennifer Regruth*

"Go ask somebody else about Jeff Gordon. I like Jeff Gordon, but I'm tired of hearing about Jeff Gordon."
—Ernie Irvan, after Gordon's strong start at Daytona in his rookie season,
Atlanta Journal and Constitution

Gordon at Atlanta Motor Speedway

Atlanta Motor Speedway has been a fickle track in the career of Jeff Gordon. Some of Gordon's best moments have come at the track, namely, clinching the 1995 and 1997 titles, but so have a steady dose of troublesome moments. Sometimes, the highs and lows have come during the same weekend. For Gordon, every good action at Atlanta seems accompanied by an equal and opposite bad reaction.

In 1992, he made his first Winston Cup start in the season-ending Hooters 500. That race is now considered one of the most important in NASCAR history, partly because it marked Gordon's debut. On the other hand, Gordon finished 31st after crashing with half the race yet to be run.

In 1995 and 1997, Gordon clinched his first two Winston Cup titles at Atlanta, propelling him into elite NASCAR company. Of course, in both instances, Gordon's effort in the title-clinching was subpar: He finished 14 laps down in 32nd place in 1995 and three laps down in 17th in 1997. Those efforts helped turn dominant seasons into championship squeakers: Gordon topped Dale Earnhardt by just 34 point in 1995, and Dale Jarrett by a mere 14 points in 1997. Along with Charlotte and Talladega, Atlanta has extracted more poor finishes out of Gordon's career than any other track (see chart).

Gordon's Atlanta Record Book—Modern Era
(min. 5 starts)

Category	Total	Rank	Modern Era Track Leader
Money Won	$947,705	7th	Dale Earnhardt—1,796,825
Career Starts	17	43rd	Darrell Waltrip—56
Total Points	2,149	39th	Dale Earnhardt—6,715
Avg. Start	12.9	12th	David Pearson—4.7
Avg. Finish	15.2	10th	Dale Earnhardt—9.5
Wins	3	6th	Dale Earnhardt—9
Winning Pct.	17.6	3rd	Bobby Labonte—25.0
Top 5s	7	17th	Dale Earnhardt—26
Top 10s	9	23rd	Dale Earnhardt—30
DNFs	4	65th	Dave Marcis—19
Poles	1	14th	Buddy Baker—5
Front Row Starts	2	19th	Dale Earnhardt—10
Laps Led	624	10th	Dale Earnhardt—2,647
Pct. Led	11.4	6th	Cale Yarborough—21.2
Races Led	10	17th	Dale Earnhardt—32
Times Led	24	19th	Dale Earnhardt—125
Times Led Most Laps	3	6th	Dale Earnhardt—9
Bonus Points	65	15th	Dale Earnhardt—205
Laps Completed	4,711	43rd	Darrell Waltrip—14,818
Pct. of Laps Completed	86.4	52nd	Steve Park—99.2
Points per Race	126.4	8th	Dale Earnhardt—146.0
Lead Lap Finishes	6	19th	Dale Earnhardt—26

Most Gordon Finishes of 30th or Worse By Track

Track	No. of Finishes
Atlanta	5
Charlotte	5
Talladega	5
Richmond	4
Rockingham	4
Texas	3

Memorable Atlanta Moments—1998 NAPA 500

Gordon capped his historic season with the best Atlanta run of his career. Overwhelming the field with a perfectly prepared car, Gordon led 113 of 221 laps under the lights and won the rain-delayed, then rain-shortened, race. Criticized for fading at the end of NASCAR's long seasons (Gordon saw large point leads shrink at the end of his 1995 and 1997 championship runs), the win was Gordon's 13th of the season, equaling the modern era mark set by Richard Petty in 1975.

Gordon Track Performance Chart

Atlanta Motor Speedway

Hampton, Georgia— 1.54 miles— 24° banking

Year	Date	Race	St.	Fin.	Total Laps	Laps Completed	Laps Led	Condition	Money	Pts.	Bonus Pts.
1992	Nov 15	Hooters 500	21	31	328	164	0	DNF— Crash	6,285	70	0
1993	Mar 20	Motorcraft Quality Parts 500	4	4	328	327	54	Running	32,000	165	5
	Nov 14	Hooters 500	15	31	328	193	6	DNF— Crash	8,710	75	5
1994	Mar 13	Purolator 500	17	8	328	326	0	Running	21,550	142	0
	Nov 13	Hooters 500	6	15	328	323	0	Running	20,125	118	0
1995	Mar 12	Purolator 500	3	1	328	328	250	Running	104,950	185	10
	Nov 12	NAPA 500	8	32	328	314	1	Running	19,975	72	5
1996	Mar 10	Purolator 500	21	3	328	328	24	Running	61,600	170	5
	Nov 10	NAPA 500	2	3	328	328	59	Running	71,600	170	5
1997	Mar 9	Primestar 500	23	42	328	59	0	DNF—Engine	34,770	37	0
	Nov 16	NAPA 500	37	17	325	322	0	Running	41,155	112	0
1998	Mar 8	Primestar 500	9	19	325	323	0	Running	44,865	106	0
	Nov 8	NAPA 500	21	1	221	221	113	Running	164,450	185	10
1999	Mar 14	Cracker Barrel 500	8	1	325	325	109	Running	117,650	185	10
	Nov 21	NAPA 500	16	38	325	181	0	DNF— Engine	59,350	49	0
2000	Mar 12	Cracker Barrel 500	7	9	325	324	4	Running	49,870	143	5
	Nov 21	NAPA 500	1	4	325	325	4	Running	88,800	165	5

Dupont crewmembers push the No. 24 Chevy to pit road for qualifying. In terms of qualifying, Atlanta is Gordon's second worst track. His average start at the D-shaped oval is 12.9, exceeded only by his 13.6 average at Talladega.

Gordon at Bristol Motor Speedway

Though he started slowly on the high-banked concrete track, Bristol has evolved into one of the most reliable Winston Cup circuits for Jeff Gordon. Between 1995 and 2000 at the .533-mile oval, Gordon scored 4 wins, 7 Top 5s, and 10 Top 10s. Even during his struggles in 2000 he ran well at Bristol, leading the most laps in the spring race (in which he finished eighth) and sticking with the leaders during the night race before engine problems dropped him from contention.

While Gordon staked his claim to the track's spring event—the Food City 500, which he won four times consecutively between 1995 and 1998—the famed Bristol night race has been less kind. In his eight nighttime attempts, Gordon has contended just once (1996 in which he finished second). Gordon's average finish in the two events best illustrates the difference in luck: 7.1 in the spring, 15.9 at night.

Despite the fact that Bristol is one of just six tracks where Gordon has yet to win a pole, qualifying has been a Gordon forte at Bristol. He has started outside of the Top 8 just twice in his career; only Bristol-legend Cale Yarborough has a better average start.

Gordon's Bristol Record Book—The Modern Era

(min. 5 starts)

Category	Total	Rank	Modern Era Track Leader
Money Won	$783,165	7th	Dale Earnhardt—1,278,381
Starts	16	41st	Darrell Waltrip—52
Total Points	2,228	30th	Darrell Waltrip—7,259.75
Avg. Start	5.5	2nd	Cale Yarborough—2.5
Avg. Finish	11.5	11th	Cale Yarborough—6.6
Wins	4	5th	Darrell Waltrip—12
Winning Pct.	25.0	3rd	Cale Yarborough—56.3
Top 5s	7	12th	Darrell Waltrip—26
Top 10s	10	18th	Darrell Waltrip—32
DNFs	4	48th	J. D. McDuffie—15
Poles	0	—	R. Wallace, Yarborough—7
Front Row Starts	6	7th	Rusty Wallace—12
Laps Led	1,281	6th	Cale Yarborough—3,872
Pct. Led	16.3	4th	Cale Yarborough—50.3
Races Led	11	13th	Earnhardt, D. Waltrip—30
Times Led	28	10th	Darrell Waltrip—94
Times Led Most Laps	3	5th	Darrell Waltrip—10
Bonus Points	70	12th	Darrell Waltrip—200
Laps Completed	7,300	33rd	Darrell Waltrip—22,964
Pct. of Laps Completed	93.1	12	Kevin Lepage—98.9
Points per Race	139.3	9th	Rusty Wallace—148.7
Fin. on Lead Lap	10	8th	Darrell Waltrip—24

Memorable Bristol Moments—1997 Food City 500

A mere 700 feet from the finish line Gordon nudged, loosened, and passed leader Rusty Wallace going into the race's final turn to win his third consecutive Bristol spring race. Wallace got revenge for that bump-and-run a year later when he sent the race-leading Gordon into the wall and out of the race at Richmond.

The 1997 Goody's 500

Memorable for the crowd's reaction rather than racing, Gordon crashed along the front stretch after being tapped by Jeremy Mayfield, bringing down a huge ovation from the large contingent of anti-Gordon fans in the stands. In the middle of another dominant season, Gordon began hearing boos in force. Ever ready to jump on Gordon, the Bristol fans began their cheers before Gordon's car had even completely spun around. By the time his car nailed the inside retaining wall, the cheers were thunderous.

Gordon Track Performance Chart

Bristol Motor Speedway

Bristol, Tennessee— .533 miles— 36° banking

Year	Date	Race	St.	Fin.	Total Laps	Laps Completed	Laps Led	Condition	Money	Pts.	Bonus Pts.
1993	Apr 4	Food City 500	21	17	500	481	0	DNF—Crash	9,400	112	0
	Aug 28	Bud 500	8	20	500	466	0	Running	11,450	103	0
1994	Apr 10	Food City 500	4	22	500	425	68	DNF—Crash	14,855	102	5
	Aug 27	Goody's 500	12	32	500	222	36	DNF—Crash	17,735	72	5
1995	Apr 2	Food City 500	2	1	500	500	205	Running	67,645	185	10
	Aug 26	Goody's 500	4	6	500	500	76	Running	27,865	155	5
1996	Mar 31	Food City 500	8	1	342	342	148	Running	83,765	185	10
	Aug 24	Goody's 500	2	2	500	500	99	Running	54,590	175	5
1997	Apr 13	Food City 500	5	1	500	500	125	Running	83,640	180	5
	Aug 23	Goody's 500	2	35	500	365	188	DNF—Crash	33,955	63	5
1998	Mar 29	Food City 500	2	1	500	500	63	Running	90,860	180	5
	Aug 22	Goody's 500	7	5	500	500	0	Running	58,650	155	0
1999	Apr 11	Food City 500	2	6	500	500	0	Running	55,970	150	0
	Aug 28	Goody's 500	4	4	500	500	48	Running	71,505	165	5
2000	Mar 26	Food City 500	3	8	500	500	225	Running	51,295	152	10
	Aug 26	Goracing.com 500	2	23	500	499	0	Running	49,985	94	0

Starting in 1995, Gordon won four consecutive spring races at Bristol, a track record. In his 1995 victory, he led 205 laps, his best effort at Bristol until leading 225 laps in the 2000 spring race. *Jennifer Regruth*

Gordon at California Speedway

Unlike the other new tracks entering the Winston Cup world, Jeff Gordon has made himself at home on the 2-mile oval in Fontana, California. In the track's four races, Gordon leads or is tied for the lead in nearly every statistical category. Among the highlights, he is the only driver to complete all 1,000 competitive laps run on the speedway and the only driver with multiple victories. And Gordon has been well paid for his efforts, taking in nearly half a million dollars—almost $140,000 better than the next best-compensated driver.

Explaining Gordon's success at California Speedway begins and ends with the track's resemblance to Michigan Speedway, which is also owned by Roger Penske. Built from the same mold (both tracks are high-speed, flat, 2-mile ovals), Michigan is one of Gordon's most consistent tracks. He and his DuPont team have successfully transferred their knowledge and race set-ups to California. The result: The California kid has found a home in Fontana.

Gordon in Inaugural Races

Track	Year	St.	Fin.	Laps Led	Money
New Hampshire	1993	3	7	3	$19,150
Indianapolis	1994	3	1	93	613,000
Texas	1997	2	30	69	60,200
California	1997	3	1	113	114,600
Las Vegas	1998	5	17	0	76,200
Homestead	1999	10	10	3	70,590
Totals (Avg.)		4.3	11.0	281	$953,740

Memorable California Moment—1997 California 500

Gordon survived a fuel-mileage contest with Mark Martin and won the inaugural event at the new speedway. Gordon completed the final 55 laps—110 miles—on a single tank of gas (raising eyebrows throughout the garage area) before running dry on the cool-down lap. The victory was Gordon's second win in five career inaugural events (the other win coming at Indianapolis).

Gordon's California Record Book—All-Time
(min. 2 starts)

Category	Total	Rank	All-Time Track Leader*
Money Won	$463,765	1st	(Bobby Labonte—326,450)
Starts	4	T-1st	26 others with 4 starts
Total Points	665	1st	(Jeremy Mayfield—633)
Avg. Start	8.8	2nd	Mark Martin—5.8
Avg. Finish	4.3	1st	(Jeremy Mayfield—5.5)
Wins	2	1st	(Martin, Mayfield—1)
Winning Pct.	50.0	1st	(Martin, Mayfield—25.0)
Top 5s	3	1st	5 tied with 2
Top 10s	3	T-1st	5 others with 3 Top 10s
DNFs	0	—	G. Bodine, Martin, Spencer—2
Poles	1	T-1st	3 others with 1 pole
Front Row Starts	1	T-1st	7 others with 1 F. R. Start
Laps Led	287	1st	(Mark Martin—193)
Pct. Led	28.7	1st	(Mark Martin—19.3)
Races Led	3	2nd	Mark Martin—4
Times Led	18	1st	(Mark Martin—14)
Times Led Most Laps	2	1st	(Kenseth, Martin—1)
Bonus Points	25	T-1st	(Mark Martin—25)
Laps Completed	1,000	1st	(Jeremy Mayfield—999)
Pct. of Laps Completed	100.0	T-1st	(Tony Stewart—100.0)
Points per Race	166.3	1st	(Jeremy Mayfield—158.3)
Fin. on Lead Lap	4	1st	8 tied with 3 Lead Lap Fin.

* Second-place driver or co-leader listed in parentheses if Gordon is track leader.

Gordon Track Performance Chart

California Speedway

Fontana, California— 2.0 miles— 14° banking

Year	Date	Race	St.	Fin.	Total Laps	Laps Completed	Laps Led	Condition	Money	Pts.	Bonus Pts.
1997	Jun 22	California 500	3	1	250	250	113	Running	$144,600	185	10
1998	May 3	California 500	1	4	250	250	23	Running	98,800	165	5
1999	May 2	California 500	5	1	250	250	151	Running	155,890	185	10
2000	Apr 30	NAPA 500	26	11	250	250	0	Running	64,475	130	0

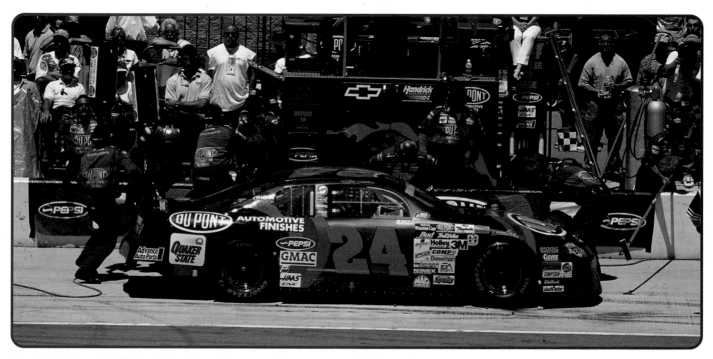

Since the first race in 1997, Gordon has shown his superspeedway prowess at the California Speedway. Leading 117 laps, he won the race in 1997, and he won it again in 1999, leading 151 laps. In this photo, the Hendrick Motorsports pit crew services Gordon's Monte Carlo for the 2000 NAPA 500, a race in which Gordon finished 11th. *Nigel Kinrade*

"That Gordon boy moves good around the track. He's extremely capable. Doesn't make dumb moves."
—Dale Earnhardt, after Gordon won his first-ever Twin 125 qualifier at Daytona, *St. Petersburg Times*

Gordon at Daytona International Speedway

A primary reason for the respect Jeff Gordon has gained among NASCAR's legendary drivers, both past and present, is his performance at Daytona International Speedway. As the capital of stock car racing, drivers who excel on the high-banked 2.5-mile track get noticed quickly. For Gordon, people began to take notice early.

In his first-ever Daytona race—the Twin 125 Qualifying event—Gordon passed veteran Bill Elliott, led more than half the race and won. In his first "real" competitive lap on the track, the first lap of the 1993 Daytona 500, Gordon scooted past pole winner Kyle Petty and Dale Jarrett and took the lead. He has built on that strong first impression ever since, claiming two poles, winning four races and a staggering $3.8 million. After 16 Daytona races, Gordon has the highest winning percent (25.0) in track history.

Gordon's Daytona Record Book—The Modern Era
(min. 5 starts)

Category	Total	Rank	Modern Era Track Leader*
Money Won	$3,811,927[1]	3rd	Dale Earnhardt—4,304,545
Starts	16	50th	Marcis, D. Waltrip—55
Total Points	2,191	35th	Dale Earnhardt—6,375
Avg. Start	10.5	8th	Bobby Isaac—4.2
Avg. Finish	12.2	3rd	Dale Earnhardt—10.7
Wins	4	5th	Richard Petty—7
Winning Pct.	25.0	1st	(David Pearson—21.7)
Top 5s	8	12th	Dale Earnhardt—22
Top 10s	10	19th	Dale Earnhardt—34
DNFs	1	149th	A.J. Foyt—23
Poles	2	9th	Cale Yarborough—8
Front Row Starts	2	18th	Cale Yarborough—13
Laps Led	336	10th	Dale Earnhardt—1,269
Pct. Led	11.8	5th	Dale Earnhardt—15.8
Races Led	12	16th	Dale Earnhardt—35
Times Led	25	19th	Dale Earnhardt—169
Times Led Most Laps	2	9th	Dale Earnhardt—7
Bonus Points	70	15th	Dale Earnhardt—210
Laps Completed	2,644	44th	Darrell Waltrip—8,482
Pct. of Laps Completed	93.2	8th	Johnny Benson—99.4
Points per Race	136.9	3rd	Dale Earnhardt—141.7
Fin. on Lead Lap	13	12th	Dale Earnhardt—28

Second-place driver or co-leader listed in parentheses if Gordon is track leader.
[1] – Money total includes 1999 No Bull Million bonus.

Memorable Daytona Moments—1999 Daytona 500

Gordon pulled what would later be called the most daring move in Daytona 500 history and then survived the challenge of restrictor-plate genius Dale Earnhardt to win his second 500. "The Move" occurred with 11 laps to go. Gordon dipped low, nearly to the tri-oval grass, to make an impossible pass on race leader Rusty Wallace. Attempting to block the move, Wallace nearly forced Gordon into the rear of Ricky Rudd's limping, damaged car on the track's apron. Wallace relented and allowed Gordon enough room to get back on the track and eventually make the pass. Gordon then held off Earnhardt in a thrilling 10-lap duel.

1998 Pepsi 400

In the first Daytona night race, Gordon outmaneuvered Jeremy Mayfield, Bobby Labonte, and Mike Skinner on the final lap, using a combination of blocking and draft-stealing maneuvers on the backstretch. Gordon kept his Chevy in front for a race-high 49 laps and won his second Pepsi 400.

Gordon Track Performance Chart

Daytona International Speedway

Daytona Beach, Florida— 2.5 miles— 31° banking

Year	Date	Race	St.	Fin.	Total Laps	Laps Completed	Laps Led	Condition	Money	Pts.	Bonus Pts.
1993	Feb 14	Daytona 500 by STP	3	5	200	200	2	Running	111,150	160	5
	Jul 3	Pepsi 400	27	5	160	160	3	Running	24,625	160	5
1994	Feb 20	Daytona 500	6	4	200	200	7	Running	112,525	165	5
	Jul 2	Pepsi 400	12	8	160	160	19	Running	25,175	147	5
1995	Feb 19	Daytona 500	4	22	200	199	61	Running	67,915	102	5
	Jul 1	Pepsi 400	3	1	160	160	72	Running	96,580	185	10
1996	Feb 18	Daytona 500	8	42	200	13	0	DNF— Handling	59,052	37	0
	Jul 6	Pepsi 400	1	3	117	117	9	Running	63,735	170	5
1997	Feb 16	Daytona 500	6	1	200	200	40	Running	456,999	180	5
	Jul 5	Pepsi 400	4	21	160	160	1	Running	85,135	105	5
1998	Feb 15	Daytona 500	29	16	200	200	56	Running	114,730	120	5
	Oct 17	Pepsi 400	8	1	160	160	49	Running	184,325	185	10
1999	Feb 14	Daytona 500	1	1	200	200	17	Running	2,172,246	180	5
	Jul 3	Pepsi 400	11	21	160	160	0	Running	56,960	100	0
2000	Feb 20	Daytona 500	11	34	200	195	0	Running	106,100	61	0
	Jul 1	Pepsi 400	34	10	160	160	0	Running	74,675	134	0

Though he has sometimes struggled to grasp restrictor-plate racing, Gordon has won six times at Daytona and Talladega, NASCAR's two restrictor-plate tracks.

In 1999, Gordon pulled what would later be called the most daring move in Daytona 500 history. He dipped low, nearly to the tri-oval grass, to make an impossible pass on race leader Rusty Wallace. Gordon then survived an 11-lap challenge from restrictor plate genius Dale Earnhardt to win his second 500.

Gordon at Dover Downs International Speedway

Like Michigan and Martinsville, Jeff Gordon needed almost no adjustment time to become comfortable with Dover Downs International Speedway. In his second start, he led 50 laps. By his fifth start he was well on his way to becoming an automatic threat to win whenever the Winston Cup series visits Delaware.

Gordon has displayed his fondness for Dover by leading laps, lots of laps. He has led more laps at Dover than at any other track in his career and his 400 laps led in the 1995 MBNA 500 is fifth in the track's single-race record book (see charts). Percentage-wise, Gordon's personal record also occurred at Dover when he led 94 percent of the 1998 MBNA Platinum 400 (during which he led 375 of 400 laps). He was at his most dominant at Dover during the four races in 1995 and 1996. He finished sixth and won three times, won two poles, and led 1,042 of 2,000 laps.

The bad news for Gordon is, while his strength at Dover has continued, victories have suddenly become difficult to secure. For instance, in the 1998 spring race, he led 375 laps but slipped to third when the race was decided by fuel-mileage considerations. The same situation occurred in the 1999 fall race. A cut right front tire ended a strong run in the spring race of 2000. Still, Gordon is one of a handful of drivers considered a threat to win every time the green flag falls on a Dover race.

Gordon's Dover Record Book—The Modern Era
(min. 5 starts)

Category	Total	Rank	Modern Era Track Leader
Money Won	$1,000,300	5th	Dale Earnhardt—1,273,660
Starts	16	46th	Marcis, D. Waltrip—53
Total Points	2,288	32nd	Darrell Waltrip—6,349
Avg. Start	7.9	5th	David Pearson—2.6
Avg. Finish	10.3	3rd	David Pearson—7.2
Wins	3	7th	Bobby Allison—6
Winning Pct.	18.8	2nd	David Pearson—35.7
Top 5s	7	18th	Dale Earnhardt—19
Top 10s	10	21st	Dale Earnhardt—25
DNFs	2	112th	J. D. McDuffie—25
Poles	2	10th	David Pearson—5
Front Row Starts	6	3rd	M. Martin, D. Pearson—8
Laps Led	1,650	8th	Bobby Allison—2,162
Pct. Led	22.6	2nd	David Pearson—28.8
Races Led	11	15th	Dale Earnhardt—26
Times Led	39	10th	Dale Earnhardt—81
Times Led Most Laps	4	6th	Cale Yarborough—6
Bonus Points	75	12th	Dale Earnhardt—150
Laps Completed	7,115	40th	Darrell Waltrip—22,539
Pct. of Laps Completed	97.5	3rd	Steve Park—99.5
Points per Race	143.0	4th	Bobby Allison—157.0
Fin. on Lead Lap	8	9th	Mark Martin—13

* Second-place driver or co-leader listed in parentheses if Gordon is track leader.

Memorable Dover Moment—1999 MBNA Gold 400

An otherwise normal Winston Cup event took on historic significance when the departure of crew chief Ray Evernham was made official. Evernham's resignation ended one of the most successful driver–crew chief teams in NASCAR history. Together, Gordon and Evernham won 3 championships, 47 races, and 30 poles. In their final race, Evernham watched Gordon quickly work his way to the front and take the lead on lap 17. A loose car and distracted race team eventually succumbed to a 17th-place finish.

Gordon Track Performance Chart

Dover Downs International Speedway

Dover, Delaware—1.0 miles— 24° banking

Year	Date	Race	St.	Fin.	Total Laps	Laps Completed	Laps Led	Condition	Money	Pts.	Bonus Pts.
1993	Jun 6	Budweiser 500	21	18	500	440	0	Running	11,485	109	0
	Sept 19	SplitFire Spark Plug 500	3	24	500	412	80	DNF—Mechanical	11,255	96	5
1994	Jun 5	Bud 500	23	5	500	500	0	Running	33,570	155	0
	Sept 18	SplitFire 500	12	11	500	499	0	Running	20,615	130	0
1995	Jun 4	Miller 500	1	6	500	499	132	Running	37,890	155	5
	Sept 17	MBNA 500	2	1	500	500	400	Running	74,655	185	10
1996	Jun 2	Miller 500	1	1	500	500	307	Running	138,730	185	10
	Sept 16	MBNA 500	3	1	500	500	203	Running	153,630	185	10
1997	Jun 1	Miller 500	2	26	500	490	18	Running	33,470	90	5
	Sept 21	MBNA 400	2	7	400	398	11	Running	38,190	151	5
1998	May 31	MBNA Platinum 400	2	3	400	400	375	Running	79,350	175	10
	Sept 20	MBNA Gold 400	6	2	400	400	6	Running	77,005	175	5
1999	Jun 6	MBNA Platinum 400	14	2	400	400	104	Running	96,805	175	5
	Sept 26	MBNA Gold 400	7	17	400	397	14	Running	49,940	117	5
2000	Jun 4	MBNA Platinum 400	19	32	400	380	0	DNF—Crash	63,420	67	0
	Sept 24	MBNA.com 400	9	9	400	400	0	Running	70,290	138	0

Gordon's Career Laps Led By Track

Track	Total Laps Led
Dover	1,650
Bristol	1,281
Martinsville	1,034
Darlington	788
Rockingham	765

Dover Record Book
Most Laps Led, Single Race

Driver	Laps Led	Year
Richard Petty	491	1974
Bobby Allison	486	1982
Dale Earnhardt	456	1989
Neil Bonnett	404	1981
Jeff Gordon	400	1995
Bill Elliott	392	1988

Steeply banked concrete tracks like Bristol and Dover have been friendly places for Jeff Gordon. Gordon has three wins at Dover and has led more laps—1,650—at the Delaware track than any other during his Winston Cup career. The second-place track? Bristol, where Gordon has led 1,281 laps.

Gordon at Homestead—Miami Speedway

Quickly becoming known as the "Pontiac Test Track" or "Joe Gibbs Raceway," the new Homestead-Miami Speedway has offered little to Chevy drivers such as Jeff Gordon. Though he finished the track's two Winston Cup events in the Top 10 (and won the Busch series event in 2000), Gordon's chances for stronger finishes have been dampened by Pontiac and Ford dominance (in 1999) and racin' luck (in 2000).

In the inaugural Homestead race, Gordon and his fellow Chevrolet competitors were overwhelmed by the superior down force of the Pontiacs and Fords, which swept the Top 5 finishing positions, including a win for rookie sensation and Gibbs driver Tony Stewart. Understanding the reality of the situation, Gordon and his team played the fuel mileage card. The trick worked enough to help Gordon take a brief lead midway through the race, but couldn't keep him on the lead lap or push him any higher than 10th in the final finishing order.

In 2000, the story seemed the same: Stewart won, Fords and Pontiacs swept the Top 6 spots, and Gordon was mired a lap off the pace. This time, however, Gordon's performance was much improved. While he was never as strong as the top two cars, he had inched his way into third when he pitted for the final time. That's when racin' luck struck. Debris on the racetrack pulled out the yellow flag three laps after Gordon's pit stop, but before leader Stewart had made his stop. Trapped a lap down, Gordon could only manage a seventh-place finish.

Gordon's Homestead Record Book—All-Time

Category	Total	Rank	All-Time Track Leader*
Money Won	$154,315	8th	Tony Stewart—569,590
Career Starts	2	T-1st	34 others with 2 Starts
Total Points	285	6th	Tony Stewart—365
Avg. Start	19.0	16th	Bobby Labonte— 3.0
Avg. Finish	8.5	6th	Tony Stewart—1.0
Wins	0	—	Tony Stewart—2
Winning Pct.	0.0	—	Tony Stewart—100.0
Top 5s	0	—	B. Labonte, M. Martin, T. Stewart—2
Top 10s	2	T-1st	(B. Labonte, M. Martin, T. Stewart—2)
DNFs	0	—	Darrell Waltrip—2
Poles	0	—	D. Green, S. Park—1
Front Row Starts	0	—	J. Andretti, D. Green, S. Park, R. Rudd—1
Laps Led	3	12th	Tony Stewart—210
Pct. Led	0.6	12th	Tony Stewart—39.3
Races Led	1	3rd	B. Labonte, T. Stewart—2
Times Led	2	4th	Tony Stewart—8
Times Led Most Laps	0	—	B. Labonte, T. Stewart—1
Bonus Points	5	3rd	B. Labonte, T. Stewart—15
Laps Completed	532	5th	B. Labonte, M. Martin, T. Stewart—534
Pct. of Laps Completed	99.6	6th	B. Labonte, M. Martin, K. Petty, T. Stewart—100.0
Points per Race	142.5	6th	Tony Stewart—182.5
Lead Lap Finishes	0	—	B. Labonte, M. Martin, T. Stewart—2

* Second-place driver or co-leader listed in parentheses if Gordon is track leader.

"Hell, in the last three or four races, he's the only car on the race track. It's unbelievable. It's completely unbelievable. It was a helluva run."
—Ward Burton, after Gordon won four straight Southern 500s at Darlington, *Winston Cup Scene*

Gordon Track Performance Chart

Homestead Motorsports Complex

Homestead, Florida— 1.5 miles— 6° banking

Year	Date	Race	St.	Fin.	Total Laps	Laps Completed	Laps Led	Condition	Money	Pts.	Bonus Pts.
1999	Nov 14	Jiffy Lube Miami 400	10	10	267	266	3	Running	$70,590	139	5
2000	Nov 12	Pennzoil 400	28	7	267	266	0	Running	83,725	146	0

While the Pontiacs have fared well at the two Homestead races run to date, Jeff Gordon and the Chevy contingent have been unable to match the sheer pace of the opposition. Nonetheless, Gordon has piloted one of the fastest Chevy's to very respectable results?a 10th in 1999 and a 7th in 2000. *Nigel Kinrade*

Gordon at Indianapolis Motor Speedway

Jeff Gordon could not have foreseen the effect that the Indianapolis Motor Speedway would have on his life when he first moved to nearby Pittsboro at age 12. Located less than 15 miles from the speedway, the small Hoosier town afforded the young Gordon a home base from which he could expand his open-wheel racing experience at an earlier age. As an open-wheel prodigy, Gordon drove the legendary Indiana tracks, Salem, Terre Haute, Winchester, and Bloomington. Many of the greats who were groomed on those short tracks later competed at Indianapolis in May.

Gordon took a separate route to Indy greatness, however. After his hyper-successful open-wheel career, he climbed into one of those lumbering stock cars and joined the Winston Cup series. In 1994, his storybook victory in the inaugural Brickyard marked his arrival as a force in the Winston Cup series and cemented his status as a big money racer.

legitimate questions can be asked about the quality of racing IMS generates when stock cars take to its hallowed track, there is little question about the prestige of the event. Even Dale Earnhardt, the quintessential old-style NASCAR racer, indicated after his 1995 Brickyard victory just how important a win at Indy was for his racing resume. In this light, no stock car driver has a more impressive resume at Indy than Gordon. He is notable at Indy for his starting (he has a track record three poles), his finishing (Gordon became the first driver to win two Brickyards) and for everything in between (he holds the track record for laps led).

Memorable Indianapolis Moment—1994 Brickyard 400

Though Gordon's win in the inaugural Indianapolis race is his second career victory, the Brickyard vaulted the 23-year-old driver into NASCAR stardom. He completed the local-boy-makes-good storybook line by surviving a late-race duel with Ernie Irvan. The victory earned Gordon a then-record payday of $613,000 and foreshadowed the great moments to come.

Gordon's Indianapolis Record Book—All-Time
(min. 3 starts)

Category	Total	Rank	All-Time Track Leader*
Money Won	$3,276,076[1]	1st	(Dale Jarrett—2,032,570)
Starts	7	T-1st	20 others with 7 starts
Total Points	981	5th	Bobby Labonte—1,039
Avg. Start	8.9	1st	(Mike Skinner—9.3)
Avg. Finish	12.1	9th	Bobby Labonte—8.1
Wins	2	T-1st	(Dale Jarrett—2)
Winning Pct.	28.6	T-1st	(Dale Jarrett—28.6)
Top 5s	4	T-1st	3 others with 4 Top 5s
Top 10s	5	2nd	Rusty Wallace—6
DNFs	1	14th	C. Little, D. Marcis—3
Poles	3	1st	(Ernie Irvan—2)
Front Row Starts	3	1st	(E. Irvan, M. Martin—2)
Laps Led	277	1st	(Dale Jarrett—186)
Pct. Led	24.7	1st	(Dale Jarrett—16.6)
Races Led	6	1st	(Earnhardt, Jarrett, Irvan—4)
Times Led	21	1st	(Dale Jarrett—11)
Times Led Most Laps	2	1st	5 tied with 1 Led Most
Bonus Points	40	1st	(E. Irvan, D. Jarrett—25)
Laps Completed	998	15th	Elliott, B. Labonte, Schrader—1,119
Pct. of Laps Completed	89.1	34th	M. Shepherd, Skinner—100.0
Points per Race	140.1	6th	Bobby Labonte—148.4
Fin. on Lead Lap	5	7th	6 with 6 Lead Lap Fin.

*Second-place driver or co-leader listed in parentheses if Gordon is track leader.
[1] – Money total includes 1998 No Bull Million bonus.

Gordon Track Performance Chart

Indianapolis Motor Speedway
Indianapolis, Indiana— 2.5 miles— 9° banking

Year	Date	Race	St.	Fin.	Total Laps	Laps Completed	Laps Led	Condition	Money	Pts.	Bonus Pts.
1994	Aug 6	Brickyard 400	3	1	160	160	93	Running	$613,000	185	10
1995	Aug 5	Brickyard 400	1	6	160	160	35	Running	299,200	155	5
1996	Aug 3	Brickyard 400	1	37	160	40	3	DNF— Crash	137,591	57	5
1997	Aug 3	Brickyard 400	24	4	160	160	25	Running	223,675	165	5
1998	Aug 1	Brickyard 400	3	1	160	160	97	Running	1,637,625	185	10
1999	Aug 7	Brickyard 400	1	3	160	160	24	Running	262,800	170	5
2000	Aug 5	Brickyard 400	29	33	160	158	0	Running	102,185	64	0

Gordon's crew works feverishly to repair the crumpled No. 24 DuPont Chevy Monte Carlo during the 1996 Brickyard 400. After starting on the pole, Gordon's car slammed into the wall after cutting a tire on lap 22. Gordon finished the race in 37th, his worst Brickyard finish in seven starts.

In one of the truly majestic settings in motorsports—the front stretch of the Indianapolis Motor Speedway on race day—Gordon completes a lap during the 1999 Brickyard 400.

Gordon at Las Vegas Motor Speedway

Las Vegas Motor Speedway, also known as "Roush Raceway," has not been kind to Jeff Gordon—or anyone else piloting something other than a Jack Roush Ford. Jeff Burton and Mark Martin, Roush racers both, have won all three Las Vegas races and have led a combined 336 or 682 laps on the track.

In the midst of this dominance, Gordon has been either overshadowed or simply a nonfactor. His best performance, a third-place finish in 1999, was background noise to that race's main story line: the down-to-the-wire battle between brothers Jeff and Ward Burton. In his two other attempts at the track, Gordon has failed to finish on the lead lap.

Hoping to improve his lot, Gordon entered the Busch races at Las Vegas in 1999 and 2000, looking for clues. While he finished fourth in 1999 Busch race, Gordon has yet to discover the secret to Roush Raceway.

Gordon's Las Vegas Record Book—All-Time
(min. 2 starts)

Category	Total	Rank	All-Time Track Leader
Money Won	$326,475	4th	Jeff Burton—898,365
Starts	3	T-1st	28 others with 3 starts
Total Points	361	9th	Jeff Burton—545
Avg. Start	8.7	5th	D. Jarrett, B. Labonte – 5.3
Avg. Finish	16.0	10th	Jeff Burton—1.3
Wins	0	—	Jeff Burton—2
Winning Pct.	0.0	—	Jeff Burton—66.7
Top 5s	1	4th	Jeff Burton—3
Top 10s	1	8th	J. Burton, Earnhardt, Martin—3
DNFs	0	—	Kenny Wallace—2
Poles	0	—	Jarrett, B. Labonte, Rudd—1
Front Row Starts	0	—	6 tied with 1 Front Row St.
Laps Led	1	21st	Jeff Burton—204
Pct. Led	.002	19th	Jeff Burton—29.9
Races Led	1	5th	J. Burton, M. Martin—3
Times Led	1	11th	Jeff Burton—11
Times Led Most Laps	0	—	Jeff Burton—2
Bonus Points	5	5th	Jeff Burton—25
Laps Completed	680	8th	4 tied with 682 Laps Comp.
Pct. of Laps Completed	99.7	9th	4 tied at 100 percent
Points per Race	120.3	10th	Jeff Burton—181.7
Fin. on Lead Lap	1	10th	4 tied with 3 Lead Lap Fin.

"Everyone is afraid of him. NASCAR is afraid of him because they can't make enough rules to stop him. The fans are afraid of him because he's squeaky clean and they can't find anything to identify with him. The competitors are afraid of him because he's going to rewrite all the records. Everybody's afraid of him and they don't appreciate him."

—Darrell Waltrip, three-time Winston Cup champion, *Winston Cup Scene*

Gordon Track Performance Chart

Las Vegas Motor Speedway

Las Vegas, Nevada— 1.5 miles— 12° banking

Year	Date	Race	St.	Fin.	Total Laps	Laps Completed	Laps Led	Condition	Money	Pts.	Bonus Pts.
1998	Mar 1	Las Vegas 400	5	17	267	266	0	Running	$76,200	112	0
1999	Mar 7	Las Vegas 400	11	3	267	267	1	Running	179,400	170	5
2000	Mar 5	Carsdirect.com 400	10	28	148	147	0	Running	70,875	79	0

Jeff Gordon has not been a serious threat at Las Vegas in the three races run at the track. Some have called Las Vegas "Roush Raceway" because Mark Martin and Jeff Burton have won all three races. Gordon took third in 1999 behind the Burton brothers, Jeff and Ward. *Nigel Kinrade*

Gordon at Lowe's Motor Speedway at Charlotte

Since moving to North Carolina to begin his Winston Cup career in 1993, Jeff Gordon has often referred to the Charlotte speedway as his home track. His performance there has done little to contradict his comfort level. In just 16 races, Gordon has quickly climbed the track's all-time lists:

· He is fifth all-time in wins with four, a total bettered only by NASCAR legends Bobby Allison (six wins), Darrell Waltrip (6), Dale Earnhardt (5), and Richard Petty (5).

· Gordon tied the great David Pearson in consecutive Coca-Cola 600 poles with five. Gordon's speed string stretched from 1994 to 1998, while Pearson's occurred from 1974 to 1978.

· Resulting from his pole success in the 600, Gordon's seven career Charlotte poles are second only to Pearson's all-time record (14).

· He is second only to Dale Earnhardt in all-time earnings, despite the fact that he has competed in 32 fewer races.

In 2000, bad luck and a missed setup resulted in an off year. Never a factor in the 600, Gordon finished 10th, then got caught up in a Rusty Wallace–Dale Jarrett accident and tied his career-low Charlotte finish in 39th.

Gordon's Charlotte Record Book—The Modern Era
(min. 5 starts)

Category	Total	Rank	Modern Era Track Leader*
Money Won	$1,731,850	2nd	Dale Earnhardt—1,933,533
Starts	16	47th	Darrell Waltrip—55
Total Points	2,082	39th	Darrell Waltrip—7,152.25
Avg. Start	7.1	2nd	David Pearson—3.8
Avg. Finish	14.7	5th	Bobby Allison—11.2
Wins	4	3rd	Darrell Waltrip—6
Winning Pct.	25.0	1st	(Davey Allison—14.3)
Top 5s	9	13th	Darrell Waltrip—19
Top 10s	10	21	Darrell Waltrip—29
DNFs	4	72nd	Dave Marcis—30
Poles	7	2nd	David Pearson—13
Front Row Starts	8	2nd	David Pearson—16
Laps Led	364	20th	Bobby Allison—1,844
Pct. Led	6.3	14th	Bobby Allison—16.3
Races Led	15	13th	Dale Earnhardt—30
Times Led	40	15th	Dale Earnhardt—120
Times Led Most Laps	0	—	Bobby Allison—8
Bonus Points	75	15th	Dale Earnhardt—175
Laps Completed	5,427	40th	Darrell Waltrip—18,239
Pct. of Laps Completed	93.5	5th	Ted Musgrave—97.4
Points per Race	130.1	11th	Bobby Allison—148.8
Fin. on Lead Lap	10	7th	Dale Earnhardt—18

* Second-place driver or co-leader listed in parentheses if Gordon is track leader.

Memorable Charlotte Moments—1994 Coca-Cola 600

In what was to become a favorite Ray Evernham gambit, Gordon took on just two tires on his final pit stop with 19 laps to go. That move allowed Gordon to maintain his lead and claim his first-ever Winston Cup win. The emotional 22-year-old driver cried in Victory Lane. As it turned out, the win was only the second biggest victory of the season for Gordon; three months later he won the inaugural Brickyard 400.

1999 UAW-GM Quality 500

Gordon won his second straight race following the departure of crew chief Evernham. Led by interim chief Brian Whitesell, Gordon patiently worked his way through the field before taking the lead for good from Bobby Labonte with just 16 laps remaining. By winning the Monday race (after being postponed for rain), Gordon finished 1999 with seven victories, leading the Winston Cup series for a record fifth-straight season.

Gordon Track Performance Chart

Lowe's Motor Speedway

Concord, North Carolina— 1.5 miles— 24° banking

Year	Date	Race	St.	Fin.	Total Laps	Laps Completed	Laps Led	Condition	Money	Pts.	Bonus Pts.
1993	May 30	Coca-Cola 600	21	2	400	400	3	Running	$79,050	175	5
	Oct 10	Mello Yello 500	1	5	334	334	1	Running	56,875	160	5
1994	May 29	Coca-Cola 600	1	1	400	400	16	Running	196,500	180	5
	Oct 9	Mello Yello 500	5	28	334	324	3	DNF—Crash	16,730	84	5
1995	May 28	Coca-Cola 600	1	33	400	283	37	DNF—Suspension	64,950	69	5
	Oct 8	UAW-GM 500	3	30	334	321	23	Running	25,915	78	5
1996	May 26	Coca-Cola 600	1	4	400	400	101	Running	118,200	165	5
	Oct 6	UAW-GM 500	2	31	334	319	14	Running	35,070	75	5
1997	May 25	Coca-Cola 600	1	1	333	333	44	Running	224,900	180	5
	Oct 5	UAW-GM Quality 500	4	5	334	334	0	Running	62,200	155	0
1998	May 24	Coca-Cola 600	1	1	400	400	53	Running	429,950	180	5
	Oct 4	UAW-GM Quality 500	26	5	334	334	47	Running	79,450	160	5
1999	May 30	Coca-Cola 600	10	39	400	341	1	DNF——Handling	56,780	51	5
	Oct 10	UAW-GM Quality 500	22	1	334	334	16	Running	140,350	180	5
2000	May 28	Coca-Cola 600	14	10	400	400	4	Running	78,950	139	5
	Oct 8	UAW-GM Quality 500	1	39	334	170	1	DNF—Crash	65,980	51	5

Jeff Gordon is fifth all-time at Charlotte in wins with four, a total bettered only by NASCAR legends Bobby Allison (six wins), Darrell Waltrip (six), Dale Earnhardt (five), and Richard Petty (five).

Gordon at Martinsville Speedway

No track on the Winston Cup circuit has been more kind to Jeff Gordon than the tight-turned .526-mile Martinsville Speedway. Gordon's consistent excellence at the short track is astonishing. With his finishes of fourth and fifth in 2000, Gordon extended his consecutive Martinsville Top 10 streak to an impressive 12 races. In only one of his 16 starts at Martinsville has Gordon finished worse than 11th. In other words, for six straight years, Gordon has never left the Virginia track with anything other than an eighth-place finish or better. He has more Top 10 finishes at Martinsville (13) than at any other track (see chart) and only Michigan accounts for more Top 5s. Only Cale Yarborough has a better career average finish at Martinsville.

Gordon's Martinsville Record Book —The Modern Era

(min. 5 starts)

Category	Total	Rank	Modern Era Track Leader*
Money Won	$834,955	4th	Dale Earnhardt—1,211,455
Starts	16	42nd	Darrell Waltrip—52
Total Points	2,479	29th	Darrell Waltrip—7,317
Avg. Start	8.4	8th	David Pearson—4.9
Avg. Finish	6.6	2nd	Cale Yarborough—6.3
Wins	3	7th	Darrell Waltrip—11
Winning Pct.	18.8	3rd	Cale Yarborough—29.4
Top 5s	10	11th	Darrell Waltrip—27
Top 10s	13	14th	Darrell Waltrip—31
DNFs	0	—	Dave Marcis—16
Poles	0	—	Darrell Waltrip—8
Front Row Starts	1	27th	Darrell Waltrip—12
Laps Led	1,034	9th	Darrell Waltrip—3,616
Pct. Led	13.2	4th	Cale Yarborough—39.9
Races Led	10	12th	Darrell Waltrip—32
Times Led	31	9th	Darrell Waltrip—79
Times Led Most Laps	2	7th	R. Wallace, Yarborough—9
Bonus Points	60	10th	Darrell Waltrip—195
Laps Completed	7,743	8th	Darrell Waltrip—23,727
Pct. of Laps Completed	98.6	1st	(Jerry Nadeau—97.7)
Points per Race	154.9	1st	(Cale Yarborough—145.8)
Fin. on Lead Lap	11	4th	Darrell Waltrip—25

* Second-place driver or co-leader listed in parentheses if Gordon is track leader.

Memorable Martinsville Moments—1997 Goody's Headache Powder 500

Gordon survived an encounter with Jimmy Spencer and went on to lead 431 of 500 laps in his second win at Martinsville. Dominant all day, Gordon was spun around by Spencer as Gordon attempted to lap him. As a result, Gordon's Chevy did a 360-degree spin coming off of Turn 4, but avoided any damaging contact with other cars or the wall. Gordon lost his lead to Bobby Hamilton, but recovered to lead the final 125 laps. Gordon's 431 laps is the second highest single-race total at Martinsville in the modern era, behind only Bobby Allison's 432 in 1972.

1999 NAPA AutoCare 500

In his first race without Ray Evernham, Gordon qualified fifth then won after he and new crew chief Brian Whitesell decided not to pit with the rest of the leaders during the race's final caution. Never a serious threat for most of the race, Gordon and Whitesell chose to stay out on the track on lap 477 while the other lead-lap car headed for the pits. That decision proved to be a great one after the strongest car, Dale Earnhardt's No. 3 Chevy, was held up by lapped cars. By the final lap, Earnhardt caught up to Gordon but could not mount a serious threat to pass.

Gordon Top 10s By Track

Track	No. of Top 10s
Martinsville	13
Michigan	12
Pocono	12
Richmond	11
Darlington	11

Gordon Track Performance Chart

Martinsville Speedway

Martinsville, Virginia— .526 miles— 12° banking

Year	Date	Race	St.	Fin.	Total Laps	Laps Completed	Laps Led	Condition	Money	Pts.	Bonus Pts.
1993	Apr 25	Hanes 500	3	8	500	497	0	Running	$11,975	142	0
	Sept 26	Goody's 500	25	11	500	498	0	Running	13,360	130	0
1994	Apr 24	Hanes 500	13	33	500	394	0	Running	10,475	64	0
	Sept 25	Goody's 500	6	11	500	499	14	Running	19,810	135	5
1995	Apr 23	Hanes 500	12	3	356	356	9	Running	36,395	170	5
	Sept 24	Goody's 500	1	7	500	500	3	Running	25,150	151	5
1996	Apr 21	Goody's 500	13	3	500	500	211	Running	57,495	175	10
	Sept 22	Hanes 500	10	1	500	500	134	Running	93,825	180	5
1997	Apr 20	Goody's 500	4	1	500	500	431	Running	99,225	185	10
	Sept 28	Hanes 500	11	4	500	500	21	Running	40,225	165	5
1998	Apr 19	Goody's 500	3	8	500	499	19	Running	47,000	147	5
	Sept 27	NAPA Autocare 500	3	2	500	500	0	Running	73,525	170	0
1999	Apr 18	Goody's 500	9	3	500	500	163	Running	71,800	170	5
	Oct 3	NAPA Autocare 500	5	1	500	500	29	Running	110,090	180	5
2000	Apr 9	Goody's 500	11	4	500	500	0	Running	65,530	160	0
	Oct 1	NAPA Autocare 500	5	5	500	500	0	Running	59,075	155	0

Martinsville Modern Era Record Book
Most Laps Led, Single Race

Driver	Laps Led	Year
Bobby Allison	432	1972
Jeff Gordon	431	1997
Rusty Wallace	409	1993
Ernie Irvan	402	1993
Ricky Rudd	380	1983

Since arriving on the scene, Gordon joined Rusty Wallace as the premier short track racers in the Winston Cup series. He's pictured here lining up next to Wallace at Bristol. Gordon's most dominating short-track effort came at Martinsville in 1997 when he led 431 laps en route to victory in the Goody's 500. Only Bobby Allison, who led 432 laps in a 1972 race, led more single-race laps in the modern era.

Gordon at Michigan International Speedway

Michigan International Speedway has been an anomaly in the career of Jeff Gordon. No track has donated as generously to Gordon's championship point totals and no one in the track's history has a better average finish (see charts). Yet, besides Phoenix, no track has been as resistant to contributing to Gordon's win column.

Not until his 12th Michigan start was Gordon able to find Victory Lane. That one victory makes Michigan unique: Gordon has multiple victories on every other long-time Winston Cup track (besides Phoenix). Of course, Gordon hasn't exactly struggled at the Brooklyn, Michigan, track. In his 16 starts, he has 11 Top 5 finishes. If getting a win has been difficult, Gordon has shown an ability to knock on the door with five second-place finishes. The 2000 season soiled Gordon's record of excellence at Michigan somewhat. With finishes of 14th and 36th, he saw his career average finish swell from 4.5 to its current 7.1.

Gordon's Michigan Record Book—The Modern Era
(min. 5 starts)

Category	Total	Rank	Modern Era Track Leader*
Money Won	$928,405	6th	Bill Elliott—1,214,383
Starts	16	47th	Dave Marcis—50
Total Points	2,486	30th	Darrell Waltrip—6,323
Avg. Start	8.9	6th	Davey Allison—5.4
Avg. Finish	7.1	1st	(Bobby Labonte—9.3)
Wins	1	13th	David Pearson—8
Winning Pct.	6.3	11th	David Pearson—33.3
Top 5s	11	10th	Cale Yarborough—18
Top 10s	12	17	Bill Elliott—27
DNFs	2	94th	Dave Marcis—18
Poles	2	4th	David Pearson—9
Front Row Starts	2	16th	Bill Elliott—11
Laps Led	514	8th	Cale Yarborough—1,152
Pct. Led	16.1	2nd	Cale Yarborough—18.1
Races Led	13	15th	Darrell Waltrip—33
Times Led	39	12th	Cale Yarborough—128
Times Led Most Laps	4	4th	Cale Yarborough—8
Bonus Points	85	10th	Darrell Waltrip—190
Laps Completed	3,132	43rd	Darrell Waltrip—8,884
Pct. of Laps Completed	98.1	4th	Kenny Irwin—98.7
Points per Race	155.4	1st	(Bobby Labonte—145.0)
Fin. on Lead Lap	13	14th	Bill Elliott—24

* Second-place driver or co-leader listed in parentheses if Gordon is track leader.

Memorable Michigan Moment—1998 Pepsi 400

Gordon drew the wrath of the Winston Cup world by beating fan-favorite Mark Martin on a restart with nine laps to go and pulling away to victory. The first career victory for Gordon at Michigan proved incredibly unpopular among fans for the following reasons:

· Martin appeared headed for victory, which would have been a soothing antidote to the recent news that his father had been killed in a plane crash.
· Gordon had taken on just two tires but seemed to be able to pull away from the dominant Martin. Two weeks later at New Hampshire, after another two-tire win by Gordon, Martin's car owner, Jack Roush, accused Gordon of cheating.
· The victory was Gordon's record-tying fourth in a row. He had won the three previous races at Pocono, Indianapolis, and Watkins Glen.

En route to a 13-win season, Gordon's win at Michigan proved to be more than many fans, and one team owner, were prepared to accept.

Gordon Track Performance Chart

Michigan Speedway

Brooklyn, Michigan— 2.0 miles—18° banking

Year	Date	Race	St.	Fin.	Total Laps	Laps Completed	Laps Led	Condition	Money	Pts.	Bonus Pts.
1993	Jun 20	Miller Genuine Draft 400	23	2	200	200	2	Running	$44,915	175	5
	Aug 15	Champion Spark Plug 400	9	3	200	200	17	Running	34,745	170	5
1994	Jun 19	Miller 400	7	12	200	200	62	Running	22,175	132	5
	Aug 21	Goodwrench 400	3	15	200	198	8	DNF— Engine	21,565	123	5
1995	Jun 18	Miller 400	1	2	200	200	80	Running	72,530	180	10
	Aug 20	Goodwrench 400	21	3	200	200	68	Running	46,420	175	10
1996	Jun 23	Miller 400	7	6	200	200	40	Running	41,650	155	5
	Aug 18	Goodwrench 400	7	5	200	200	0	Running	44,040	155	0
1997	Jun 15	Miller 400	12	5	200	200	0	Running	47,425	155	0
	Aug 17	DeVilbiss 400	17	2	200	200	1	Running	85,728	175	5
1998	Jun 14	Miller Lite 400	4	3	200	200	132	Running	84,375	175	10
	Aug 16	Pepsi 400	3	1	200	200	9	Running	120,302	180	5
1999	Jun 13	Kmart 400	1	2	200	200	20	Running	90,050	175	5
	Aug 22	Pepsi 400	9	2	200	200	73	Running	83,030	180	10
2000	Jun 11	Kmart 400	3	14	194	193	2	Running	47,250	126	5
	Aug 20	Pepsi 400	16	36	200	141	0	DNF— Handling	42,205	55	0

Best Average Finish at Michigan

(min. 5 starts)

Driver	Avg. Finish
Jeff Gordon	7.1
Bobby Labonte	9.3
Cale Yarborough	10.3
Bobby Allison	11.5
David Pearson	11.5

Most Championship Points Earned By Jeff Gordon By Track

Track	Total Points
Michigan	2,486
Martinsville	2,479
Darlington	2,351
Pocono	2,338
Dover	2,288

No track has contributed to Jeff Gordon's championship points total more than Michigan. Thanks to his consistency, no driver in track history has a better average finish.

Gordon's New Hampshire Record Book—All-Time

(min. 5 starts)

Category	Total	Rank	All-Time Track Leader*
Money Won	$1,119,890	1st	(Jeff Burton—914,490)
Starts	12	T-1st	16 others with 12 Starts
Total Points	1,717	2nd	Mark Martin—1,796
Avg. Start	11.1	5th	Ken Schrader—6.8
Avg. Finish	10.7	3rd	Mark Martin—7.8
Wins	3	2nd	Jeff Burton—4
Winning Pct.	25.0	2nd	Jeff Burton—33.3
Top 5s	7	T-1st	(J. Burton, M. Martin—7)
Top 10s	9	2nd	Mark Martin—10
DNFs	2	7th	Andretti, T. Labonte—5
Poles	2	T-1st	4 others with 2 Poles
Front Row Starts	4	1st	(Hamilton, R. Wallace—3)
Laps Led	529	2nd	Jeff Burton—593
Pct. Led	14.8	2nd	Jeff Burton—16.6
Races Led	8	1st	(B. Labonte, D. Jarrett—7)
Times Led	23	1st	(Ernie Irvan—14)
Times Led Most Laps	3	T-1st	(Jeff Burton—3)
Bonus Points	55	1st	(Jeff Burton—40)
Laps Completed	3,384	9th	Dale Earnhardt—3,565
Pct. of Laps Completed	94.7	16th	Johnny Benson—99.8
Points per Race	143.1	2nd	Mark Martin—149.7
Fin. on Lead Lap	9	2nd	Mark Martin—10

* Second-place driver or co-leader listed in parentheses if Gordon is track leader.

Memorable New Hampshire Moment— 1998 Dura Lube/Kmart 300

Gordon and Evernham pulled their patented two-tire pit stop gambit with 65 laps remaining and drove away from Mark Martin for the win. The victory set off a firestorm soon to be called "Tiregate" as Jack Roush, Martin's car owner, angrily demanded a full inspection of the tires used by Gordon and his team. Martin had dominated the race prior to Gordon's fateful two-tire stop. Despite taking on four tires, conventionally considered the better choice, Martin saw Gordon and his two fresh tires pull away and eventually win by more than half a second.

As it turned out, New Hampshire was simply the impetus for Roush to express his general rage against the Gordon-Evernham machine. Roush claimed to have proof that Gordon's team was using an illegal substance to treat, or soak, its tires. In Roush's theory, the substance softened the tires, allowing Gordon's car to grip the track better than cars using untreated tires. This heightened grip allowed Gordon to drive his car deeper into the corners, and therefore pull away from the field. In the midst of one of the greatest seasons in NASCAR history, Gordon was the target of many conspiracy theories as to how he and his team could so thoroughly dominate the competitive Winston Cup series.

NASCAR responded to Roush's claims by immediately confiscating Gordon's car and tires. Gordon's car was completely torn down and inspected. Meanwhile, the tires were sent to a lab and reverse-engineered "back to the rubber tree" in an attempt to discover foul play. When it became apparent that nothing illegal could be found in Gordon's tires and no illegal softening agent could be detected, Roush's claim became even more fanciful: The softening agent is so subtle, he posited, that it cannot be detected during inspection. In other words, Roush had created the perfect crime: The illegal substance worked well enough to help Gordon "steal" wins, but any evidence of wrongdoing disappeared, leaving NASCAR and its labs powerless to catch and punish the offenders.

With the waters muddied by Roush's unproved, and apparently improvable, claim, NASCAR reacted by changing procedures relating to tires at the tracks. NASCAR now impounds tires overnight, allowing the team to possess their allotted rubber only during practice sessions, qualifying, and the race itself.

Gordon's reaction to the controversy? He won four more races and extended his lead over Roush and Martin from 67 point to 364 en route to his third Winston Cup title.

Gordon Track Performance Chart

New Hampshire International Speedway

Loudon, New Hampshire— 1.058 miles— 12° banking

Year	Date	Race	St.	Fin.	Total Laps	Laps Completed	Laps Led	Condition	Money	Pts.	Bonus Pts.
1993	Jul 11	Slick 50 300	3	7	300	300	3	Running	$19,150	151	5
1994	Jul 10	Slick 50 300	2	39	300	160	9	DNF— Crash	22,100	51	5
1995	Jul 9	Slick 50 300	21	1	300	300	126	Running	160,300	185	10
1996	Jul 14	Jiffy Lube 300	16	34	300	253	59	DNF— Ignition	35,875	71	10
1997	Jul 13	Jiffy Lube 300	29	23	300	298	0	Running	37,975	94	0
	Sept 14	CMT 300	13	1	300	300	137	Running	188,625	185	10
1998	Jul 12	Jiffy Lube 300	2	3	300	300	73	Running	116,025	170	5
	Aug 30	Farm Aid on CMT 300	1	1	300	300	68	Running	205,400	180	5
1999	Jul 11	Jiffy Lube 300	1	3	300	300	54	Running	97,050	170	5
	Sept 19	Dura Lube/Kmart 300	19	5	300	300	0	Running	88,440	155	0
2000	Jul 9	Thatlook.com 300	8	5	273	273	0	Running	74,375	155	0
	Sept 17	Dura Lube 300	18	6	300	300	0	Running	74,575	150	0

One of the most electrifying races of the 2001 season was the New England 300. The No. 24 car captured the pole and was sitting in third late in the race when second place Dale Jarrett nudged aside Yates Racing teammate Ricky Rudd to take the lead. Gordon capitalized on the opportunity to take second from the out-of-position Rudd, and eventually finished in the runner up spot behind the incredibly strong-running Jarrett. *Nigel Kinrade*

Gordon at North Carolina Speedway

The first time Jeff Gordon climbed into a heavy stock car, a machine worlds apart from the nimble sprint cars he was used to, he did so in a driving school at the North Carolina Speedway in Rockingham. Surprisingly, that initial experience hasn't helped the quick-learning Gordon very much.

Besides the still-new Texas Motor Speedway, Rockingham is Gordon's worst track (see charts). By itself, The Rock accounts for 11 percent of Gordon's DNFs.

Despite the bad news, Gordon can point to one magical stretch during the 1997 and 1998 seasons in which Rockingham was especially generous. Gordon won three of the four races during those two seasons and finished in fourth in the other race. Based mainly on the strength of that run, Gordon's four career victories put him fifth all-time at NCS. And while he has trouble finishing races there, qualifying on the high-banked, 1.017-mile track has never been difficult for Gordon. His 6.3 average start is the best at Rockingham in the modern era.

Memorable Rockingham Moment—1998 AC Delco 400

After struggling to solidify his grip on Winston Cup championships in 1995 and 1997, Gordon put all doubts to rest with a come-from-behind win that clinched his third title. Gordon had allowed comfortable point leads to evaporate with lackluster season-ending performances. That changed in 1998 at Rockingham, marking the first time Gordon got to celebrate the championship somewhere other than the season-closing race at Atlanta.

Worst Average Finish By Track

Track	Average Finish
Texas	32.3
Rockingham	16.1
Las Vegas	16.0
Atlanta	15.9
Talladega	15.2

Most DNFs By Track

Track	DNFs
Rockingham	5
Atlanta	4
Bristol	4
Charlotte	4
Talladega	4

Most Finishes Outside of Top 10 By Track

Track	Nontop 10s
Rockingham	9
Atlanta	8
Talladega	8

Gordon's Rockingham Record Book—The Modern Era
(min. 5 starts)

Category	Total	Rank	Modern Era Track Leader*
Money Won	$893,185	4th	Dale Earnhardt—1,160,755
Career Starts	16	45th	Darrell Waltrip—56
Total Points	1,977	41st	Darrell Waltrip—6,993.5
Avg. Start	6.3	1st	(Davey Allison—7.0)
Avg. Finish	16.1	23rd	Cale Yarborough—10.8
Wins	4	4th	R. Petty, C. Yarborough — 6
Winning Pct.	25.0	2nd	David Pearson—26.7
Top 5s	6	16th	Darrell Waltrip—19
Top 10s	7	27th	Darrell Waltrip—29
DNFs	5	45th	B. Baker, J. D. McDuffie—18
Poles	1	17th	M. Martin, K. Petty—5
Front Row Starts	2	20th	Mark Martin—8
Laps Led	765	14th	Cale Yarborough—2,902
Pct. Led	11.3	4th	David Pearson—23.1
Races Led	11	16th	Dale Earnhardt—29
Times Led	36	14th	Cale Yarborough—93
Times Led Most Laps	1	13th	Cale Yarborough—9
Bonus Points	60	19th	Dale Earnhardt—155
Laps Completed	6,255	45th	Darrell Waltrip—24,031
Pct. of Laps Completed	92.2	17th	Kenny Irwin—99.1
Points per Race	123.6	28th	Cale Yarborough—148.8
Lead Lap Finishes	6	15th	Dale Earnhardt—16

* Second-place driver or co-leader listed in parentheses if Gordon is track leader.

Gordon Track Performance Chart

North Carolina Motor Speedway

Rockingham, North Carolina— 1.017 miles— 22–25° banking

Year	Date	Race	St.	Fin.	Total Laps	Laps Completed	Laps Led	Condition	Money	Pts.	Bonus Pts.
1993	Feb 28	GM Goodwrench 500	28	34	492	402	0	DNF— Engine	$6,700	61	0
	Oct 24	AC-Delco 500	7	21	492	486	0	Running	11,350	100	0
1994	Feb 27	Goodwrench 500	3	32	492	462	0	DNF— Crash	13,500	67	0
	Oct 23	AC-Delco 500	15	29	492	437	101	DNF— Mechanical	26,300	81	5
1995	Feb 26	Goodwrench 500	1	1	492	492	329	Running	167,600	185	10
	Oct 22	AC-Delco 400	4	20	393	391	57	Running	25,550	108	5
1996	Feb 25	Goodwrench 400	2	40	393	134	0	DNF—Engine	31,730	43	0
	Oct 20	AC-Delco 400	3	12	393	392	1	Running	35,000	132	5
1997	Feb 23	Goodwrench Service 400	4	1	393	393	43	Running	93,115	180	5
	Oct 27	AC-Delco 400	5	4	393	393	23	Running	41,150	165	5
1998	Feb 22	Goodwrench Service Plus 400	4	1	393	393	73	Running	90,090	180	5
	Nov 1	AC-Delco 400	9	1	393	393	29	Running	111,575	180	5
1999	Feb 21	North Carolina 400	3	39	393	310	89	DNF——Engine	44,125	51	5
	Oct 24	Pop Secret Popcorn 400	4	11	393	392	0	Running	50,790	130	0
2000	Feb 27	Dura Lube/Kmart 400	5	10	393	392	16	Running	61,510	139	5
	Oct 22	Pop Secret Popcorn 400	3	2	393	393	4	Running	83,100	175	5

The Dupont crew tends to the No. 24 Chevy on pit road at Rockingham in 1998. In 16 races at The Rock, Gordon has started outside of the Top 10 just twice. He has four wins at the track.

Gordon takes the middle line at Rockingham during the 2000 Dura Lube/Kmart 400. More than most other drivers, Gordon has shown a willingness to test a variety of lines around the banked track. In recent races, he has allowed the No. 24 Chevy to drift up to the wall between turns 3 and 4. The result in 2000 was consecutive Top-10 finishes, including second in the fall race.

Gordon at North Wilkesboro Speedway

Though North Wilkesboro Speedway disappeared from the Winston Cup schedule early in Jeff Gordon's career, his performance at the track aptly mirrors the young phenom's rise in the sport.

During his rookie season in 1993, Gordon suffered through 11 DNFs. Two of them came at North Wilkesboro. In his first trip to the .625-mile track, Gordon crashed and was gone from the race by lap 25. That race accounts for Gordon's smallest-ever Winston Cup paycheck, $4,180 for finishing 34th. By 1996, however, Gordon was well on his way to becoming the circuit's most dominant driver. His win in the track's final race, the Tyson/Holly Farms 400 in the fall of 1996, was his 10th of the season and began a string of three consecutive 10-victory seasons.

In between the initial low and the ultimate high was a rapidly improving performance. In 1993's second North Wilkesboro race, Gordon again finished 34th. He followed with a 15th and an 8th in 1994, then closed with four straight Top 3 finishes.

Gordon doesn't very well fit the Winston Cup mold off the track. But his ability to adapt to and conquer one of the oldest, most revered Winston Cup venues indicates that, on the track, he's from the same mold as Petty, Waltrip, and Earnhardt.

Gordon's North Wilkesboro Record Book —The Modern Era

(min. 5 starts)

Category	Total	Rank	Modern Era Track Leader
Money Won	$278,600	15th	Dale Earnhardt—853,685
Career Starts	8	58th	Dave Marcis—46
Total Points	1,082	54th	Darrell Waltrip—6,435.75
Avg. Start	10.1	10th	Cale Yarborough—3.9
Avg. Finish	12.4	16th	Cale Yarborough—5.7
Wins	1	10th	Darrell Waltrip—10
Winning Pct.	12.5	5th	Cale Yarborough—31.2
Top 5s	4	19th	Dale Earnhardt—21
Top 10s	5	29th	Dale Earnhardt—32
DNFs	2	46th	J. D. McDuffie—16
Poles	1	15th	Darrell Waltrip—9
Front Row Starts	2	16th	Darrell Waltrip—13
Laps Led	314	15th	Darrell Waltrip—2,923
Pct. Led	9.8	6th	Cale Yarborough—25.1
Races Led	3	22nd	Earnhardt, D. Waltrip— 24
Times Led	12	14th	Darrell Waltrip—65
Times Led Most Laps	1	11th	R. Petty, D. Waltrip— 8
Bonus Points	20	20th	Darrell Waltrip—160
Laps Completed	2,536	59th	Darrell Waltrip—17,370
Pct. of Laps Completed	79.3	61st	Ken Schrader—99.2
Points per Race	135.3	9th	Dale Earnhardt—156.4
Fin. on Lead Lap	4	19th	Dale Earnhardt—22

Memorable North Wilkesboro Moment—1996 Tyson 400

Gordon once again showed his uncanny ability to insert himself into NASCAR history. He was there for Richard Petty's final race in 1992 (which was Gordon's first Winston Cup race), he won the first stock car race at the hallowed Indianapolis Motor Speedway, and in 1996 he won the final race at one of NASCAR's original tracks. The first North Wilkesboro race occurred in NASCAR's first season, 1949. In its 97th and final race in 1996, Gordon etched his name in the legendary track's record book with a dominating victory. Leading 207 of 400 laps, he crossed the finish line two seconds ahead of one of the all-time best North Wilkesboro drivers, Dale Earnhardt.

"All you hear about these days is people talking about being steady, collecting points. To hell with that. I went out there to win …, and the kid does, too. He's a throwback."
—Cale Yarborough, *ESPN Magazine*

Gordon Track Performance Chart

North Wilkesboro Speedway

North Wilkesboro, North Carolina— .625 miles— 14° banking

Year	Date	Race	St.	Fin.	Total Laps	Laps Completed	Laps Led	Condition	Money	Pts.	Bonus Pts.
1993	Apr 18	First Union 400	7	34	400	25	0	DNF— Crash	4,180	61	0
	Oct 3	Tyson/Holly Farms 400	16	34	400	117	0	DNF—Mechanical	5,655	61	0
1994	Apr 17	First Union 400	12	15	400	396	0	Running	13,100	118	0
	Oct 2	Tyson 400	12	8	400	398	0	Running	16,875	142	0
1995	Apr 9	First Union 400	1	2	400	400	95	Running	61,625	175	5
	Oct 1	Tyson 400	14	3	400	400	12	Running	33,065	170	5
1996	Apr 14	First Union 400	17	2	400	400	0	Running	52,750	170	0
	Sept 29	Tyson 400	2	1	400	400	207	Running	91,350	185	10

Gordon leads the field on to the track for the 1995 First Union 400 at North Wilkesboro. Surrounding him are Brett Bodine (No. 11 Lowe's), Derrike Cope (No. 12 Mane 'n Tail), and Bobby Hamilton (No. 43 STP). Gordon went on to finish second to Dale Earnhardt in the race. Gordon won the 97th and final Winston Cup race ever held at North Wilkesboro in 1996.

Gordon at Phoenix International Raceway

Phoenix International Raceway is the last hold out, the final track that has yet to give into the talents of Jeff Gordon. Of the 18 tracks that have been a part of the Winston Cup circuit for an appreciable amount of time during his career, Gordon has failed to win only at Phoenix. The brand-new tracks at Texas, Las Vegas, and Homestead (Winston Cup tracks for less than five years) remain unconquered territory.

Despite Phoenix's persistent resistance, Gordon has enjoyed success at the desert track. In his eight races there, he has finished 10th or better six times. Indeed, while Gordon attempted—and often struggled—to close out championships between 1995 and 1998, Phoenix was rarely an inhibitor. In 1995, Gordon finished fifth, followed by a fifth in 1996 and seventh in 1998. Only in 1997, when he finished 17th, did Phoenix contribute to Gordon's late-season woes.

Gordon's Phoenix Record Book—All-Time
(min. 5 starts)

Category	Total	Rank	All-Time Track Leader
Money Won	$349,970	8th	Mark Martin— 603,460
Career Starts	8	25th	11 tied with 13 Starts
Total Points	1,076	18th	Mark Martin—1,982
Avg. Start	11.9	5th	Rusty Wallace—5.0
Avg. Finish	11.3	6th	Alan Kulwicki—5.2
Wins	0	—	Davey Allison— 2
Winning Pct.	0.0	—	Davey Allison—40.0
Top 5s	3	7th	Mark Martin—7
Top 10s	6	4th	Mark Martin—11
DNFs	1	27th	Dick Trickle—5
Poles	0	—	Rusty Wallace— 3
Front Row Starts	1	6th	Rusty Wallace—5
Laps Led	49	17th	Rusty Wallace— 777
Pct. Led	2.0	16th	Rusty Wallace—19.4
Races Led	2	17th	M. Martin, R. Wallace— 9
Times Led	2	21st	M. Martin, R. Wallace—20
Times Led Most Laps	0	—	Rusty Wallace— 3
Bonus Points	10	19th	Rusty Wallace— 60
Laps Completed	2,321	26th	Terry Labonte— 3,995
Pct. of Laps Completed	95.1	19th	Alan Kulwicki—100.0
Points per Race	134.5	6th	Alan Kulwicki —160.0
Lead Lap Finishes	5	7th	Mark Martin —11

Memorable Phoenix Moment—1998 Dura-Lube 500

Rain shortened the Dura Lube/Kmart 500 to 257 of its scheduled 312 laps. *Rain.* In *Phoenix.* Thanks to the uncharacteristic weather, Gordon lost a chance at history. Entering the race, he had finished 17 consecutive races in the Top 5, one race shy of tying David Pearson's all-time record of 18. Though Gordon did not seem poised to win, he showed signs that a Top 5 finish was possible. Instead, the rain fell, locking Gordon into his seventh-place standing. He followed the Phoenix race with wins at Rockingham and Atlanta, and what could have been a record-shattering 20 straight Top 5s.

Gordon Track Performance Chart

Phoenix International Raceway

Phoenix, Arizona— 1.0 mile— 9–11° banking

Year	Date	Race	St.	Fin.	Total Laps	Laps Completed	Laps Led	Condition	Money	Pts.	Bonus Pts.
1993	Oct 31	Slick 50 500	9	35	312	195	48	DNF— Mechanical	$7,610	63	5
1994	Oct 30	Slick 50 300	14	4	312	311	1	Running	26,780	165	5
1995	Oct 29	Dura-Lube 500K	3	5	312	312	0	Running	33,580	155	0
1996	Oct 27	Dura-Lube 500K	19	5	312	312	0	Running	45,065	155	0
1997	Nov 2	Dura-Lube 500	12	17	312	310	0	Running	29,880	112	0
1998	Oct 25	Dura-Lube 500	12	7	257	257	0	Running	47,040	146	0
1999	Nov 7	Checker/Dura Lube 500	2	10	312	312	0	Running	78,465	134	0
2000	Nov 5	Checker/Dura Lube 500	24	7	312	312	0	Running	81,550	146	0

Phoenix has been a fixture on the NASCAR schedule since Gordon entered the Winston Cup In 1993, and the three-time champion has failed to find the victory groove. While Gordon hasn't topped the standings at this track, he has posted 6 top 10 finishes and collected a lot of points in the process. In his eight race starts, his average finish is fifth.
Nigel Kinrade

"[DuPont] earns $5 for every $1 [spent] on the Gordon team. … 'This has been magnificent for us, absolutely phenomenal,' says Lou Savelli, president of DuPont's automotive-finishes division. 'He's helped us keep our current business and obtain new business. In three or four years, the deal paid for itself.'"
—Roy S. Johnson, *Fortune Magazine*

Gordon at Pocono Raceway

For Jeff Gordon, the learning curve at Pocono Raceway resembles a gentle slope. Besides poor finishes in his rookie season, Gordon has displayed little trouble in figuring out the flat, triangular superspeedway.

In 14 Pocono races between 1994 and 2000, Gordon compiled eight Top 3 finishes and 12 Top 10s. Since he joined the Winston Cup circuit in 1993, no driver has led as many Pocono laps (see chart). The best illustration of Gordon's comfort level is an eight-race stretch from 1995 to 1999, during which he finished first or second seven times. Gordon is the all-time track leader in average finish and points per race. Even in his subpar 2000 season, Gordon performed well at Pocono, finishing eighth and third in the track's two races.

Memorable Pocono Moments—1995 UAW-GM 500

In an early sign that even dominant drivers are human too, race-leading Gordon missed a shift on the race's final restart with just seven laps to go. Losing all momentum, Gordon watched eventual race winner Terry Labonte and 14 other cars stream past him. Gordon recovered but finished the race in 16th spot. Gordon had dominated the race, leading 124 laps.

1998 Pennsylvania 500

Once again dominant on the 2.5-mile track, Gordon suddenly felt insecure about his chances when Dale Earnhardt bumped his car coming off the track's Tunnel Turn on lap 136. Earnhardt got underneath Gordon's back bumper hard enough to lift the No. 24 car's rear wheels off the track. The contact slid Gordon out of the groove and allowed Earnhardt to pass. Gordon recovered, led 164 of 200 laps and won the race by more than a second.

Most Laps Led at Pocono (since 1993)

Driver	Laps Led
Jeff Gordon	574
Rusty Wallace	442
Dale Jarrett	405
Mark Martin	225
Geoffrey Bodine	187

Gordon's Pocono Record Book—All-Time

(min. 5 starts)

Category	Total	Rank	All-Time Track Leader*
Money Won	$1,069,235	2nd	Dale Earnhardt— 1,089,420
Starts	16	38th	Darrell Waltrip—44
Total Points	2,338	23rd	Darrell Waltrip—5,286
Avg. Start	7.6	4th	David Pearson—4.7
Avg. Finish	9.8	1st	(Davey Allison—9.77)
Wins	3	5th	Elliott, Richmond, R. Wallace, D. Waltrip— 4
Winning Pct.	18.8	2nd	Tim Richmond— 28.6
Top 5s	8	10th	H. Gant, M. Martin — 14
Top 10s	12	13th	Dale Earnhardt— 22
DNFs	2	72nd	Dave Marcis—15
Poles	2	7th	Ken Schrader—5
Front Row Starts	3	11th	Ken Schrader—8
Laps Led	574	4th	Geoffrey Bodine—809
Pct. Led	17.9	2nd	David Pearson—27.8
Races Led	12	15th	Dale Earnhardt—24
Times Led	42	11th	Darrell Waltrip—106
Times Led Most Laps	3	3rd	Geoffrey Bodine— 6
Bonus Points	75	11th	Geoffrey Bodine—145
Laps Completed	2,947	36th	Terry Labonte—7,502
Pct. of Laps Completed	92.1	22nd	Kevin Lepage—99.8
Points per Race	146.1	1st	Tim Richmond— 144.4
Fin. on Lead Lap	12	13th	Dale Earnhardt—23

* Second-place driver or co-leader listed in parentheses if Gordon is track leader.

"Sure, he's got a lot of raw talent, but I can't see where he's any greater than Bobby Labonte. Jeff's been real fortunate with the opportunities he's been given. He's on a good team and he's got a crew chief [Ray Evernham] that's probably very underrated."

—Ricky Rudd, Winston Cup driver, *Arizona Republic*

Gordon Track Performance Chart

Pocono Raceway

Long Pond, Pennsylvania— 2.5 miles— 6–14° banking

Year	Total Date	Laps Race	St.	Fin.	Total Laps	Laps Completed	Laps Led	Condition	Money	Pts.	Bonus Pts.
1993	Jun 13	Champion Spark Plug 500	4	28	200	113	0	Running	$8,535	79	0
	Jul 18	Miller Genuine Draft 500	20	37	200	49	0	DNF—Engine	9,615	52	0
1994	Jun 12	UAW-GM 500	4	6	200	200	2	Running	23,505	155	5
	Jul 17	Miller 500	7	8	200	199	0	Running	21,760	142	0
1995	Jun 11	UAW-GM 500	5	16	200	200	124	Running	38,655	125	10
	Jul 16	Miller 500	11	2	200	200	18	Running	48,520	175	5
1996	Jun 16	UAW-GM 500	1	1	200	200	94	Running	96,980	185	10
	Jul 21	Miller 500	15	7	200	200	1	Running	35,825	151	5
1997	Jun 8	Pocono 500	11	1	200	200	59	Running	166,080	180	5
	Jul 20	Pennsylvania 500	6	2	200	200	53	Running	56,745	175	5
1998	Jun 21	Pocono 500	1	2	200	200	17	Running	79,500	175	5
	Jul 26	Pennsylvania 500	2	1	200	200	164	Running	165,495	185	10
1999	Jun 20	Pocono 500	17	2	200	200	10	Running	111,220	175	5
	Jul 25	Pennsylvania 500	7	32	200	186	22	DNF—Suspension	49,990	72	5
2000	Jun 18	Pocono 500	5	8	200	200	0	Running	64,765	142	0
	Jul 23	Pennsylvania 500	5	3	200	200	10	Running	92,045	170	5

Gordon has certainly been dialed into the Pennsylvania's Pocono Raceway. Despite two mechanical DNFs, the No. 24 pilot has collected 12 top 10s in 16 starts. Let us not overlook the fact that he has won the race three times.
Nigel Kinrade

Gordon at Richmond International Raceway

Along with Martinsville, Michigan, and Pocono, Richmond International Raceway has proven to be one of Gordon's steadiest tracks. Though his performance at Richmond cannot be called spectacular (he has a relatively modest two victories in 16 starts) it can be called spectacularly consistent.

In Gordon's first 12 races at the track, he finished outside of the Top 10 just two times. One of those uncharacteristic finishes was compliments of Rusty Wallace, who in the 1998 spring race knocked the race-leading Gordon into the wall and out of the race. Gordon ended in 37th that day, his second worst finish ever at Richmond.

Lately, mirroring Gordon's recent struggles, Richmond has been less kind. In 1999, Gordon finished 31st and 40th in his two Richmond races, then followed with a ho-hum 14th in the first race of 2000. His strong run in the second 2000 race, a win tainted by postrace inspection problems, seemed to signal a return to steadiness.

Memorable Richmond Moments —2000 Chevrolet Monte Carlo 400

Strong, but not a race leader all night, Gordon overtook Jeff Burton on a restart with 15 laps to go and won his second Richmond trophy. The celebration died down later, however, when post-race inspection revealed Gordon's team used an unapproved part, a magnesium intake manifold rather than the approved aluminum model. NASCAR fined crew chief Robbie Loomis and penalized Gordon 100 points in the championship standings, marking the first time Gordon ever had points taken away. The Gordon camp argued that the same part had passed inspection throughout the season and was used by other teams. But these arguments were rejected by NASCAR officials.

1998 Exide Batteries 400

Reprising their classic showdown in the 1997 Southern 500, Gordon and Jeff Burton battled all night and ended the race in a thrilling side-by-side fight during the final five laps. Holding the quicker outside line, Burton fended off Gordon's challenge and won the race by a mere .051 seconds. Before their final-lap skirmish, Gordon and Burton swapped the lead nine times. Burton built a one-second lead with 18 laps to go before Gordon began closing. Gordon caught the leader with five to go, initiating the memorable race-closing battle.

Gordon's Richmond Record Book—The Modern Era
(min. 5 starts)

Category	Total	Rank	Modern Era Track Leader
Money Won	$833,005	8th	Dale Earnhardt—1,272,235
Starts	16	40th	Darrell Waltrip—51
Total Points	2,090	22nd	Darrell Waltrip—7,062
Avg. Start	6.9	3rd	Benny Parsons—5.2
Avg. Finish	12.4	13th	Bobby Allison—7.8
Wins	2	8th	B. Allison, R. Petty, R. Wallace, D. Waltrip— 6
Winning Pct.	12.5	6th	Bobby Allison—20.0
Top 5s	8	12th	Dale Earnhardt—25
Top 10s	11	16th	D. Earnhardt, D. Waltrip— 33
DNFs	3	51st	J. D. McDuffie—12
Poles	3	3rd	Bobby Allison— 8
Front Row Starts	7	3rd	Darrell Waltrip—14
Laps Led	546	13th	Richard Petty— 2,570
Pct. Led	8.5	10th	Bobby Allison— 20.5
Races Led	12	8th	Darrell Waltrip— 27
Times Led	29	8th	Dale Earnhardt—72
Times Led Most Laps	2	7th	B. Allison, R. Wallace—7
Bonus Points	70	8th	Darrell Waltrip—165
Laps Completed	6,053	38th	Darrell Waltrip—18,741
Pct. of Laps Completed	94.6	16th	Ted Musgrave—99.4
Points per Race	130.6	15th	Bobby Allison—152.3
Lead Lap Finishes	11	9th	Dale Earnhardt—25

Gordon Track Performance Chart

Richmond International Raceway

Richmond, Virginia— .750 miles— 14° banking

Year	Date	Race	St.	Fin.	Total Laps	Laps Completed	Laps Led	Condition	Money	Pts.	Bonus Pts.
1993	Mar 7	Pontiac Excitement 400	8	6	400	400	0	Running	$14,700	150	0
	Sept 11	Miller Genuine Draft 400	22	10	400	400	0	Running	14,205	134	0
1994	Mar 6	Pontiac Excitement 400	8	3	400	400	2	Running	34,000	170	5
	Sept 10	Miller 400	13	2	400	400	2	Running	40,365	175	5
1995	Mar 5	Pontiac Excitement 400	1	36	400	183	1	DNF— Fuel Pump	28,750	60	5
	Sept 9	Miller 400	2	6	400	400	63	Running	38,255	155	5
1996	Mar 3	Pontiac Excitement 400	2	1	400	400	124	Running	92,400	180	10
	Sept 7	Miller 400	2	2	400	400	168	Running	59,640	180	10
1997	Mar 26	Pontiac Excitement 400	2	4	400	399	65	Running	46,200	165	5
	Sept 6	Exide Batteries 400	10	3	400	400	0	Running	52,355	165	0
1998	Jun 6	Pontiac Excitement 400	1	37	400	372	2	DNF— Crash	44,975	57	5
	Sept 12	Exide Batteries 400	5	2	400	400	30	Running	85,190	175	5
1999	May 15	Pontiac Excitement 400	1	31	400	388	18	Running	54,275	75	5
	Sept 11	Exide Batteries 400	6	40	400	311	56	DNF— Transmission	50,625	48	5
2000	May 6	Pontiac Excitement 400	15	14	400	400	0	Running	46,850	121	0
	Sept 9	Chevrolet Monte Carlo 400	13	1	400	400	15	Running	130,220	80	5

One of the most famous wrecks of Gordon's career came at Richmond in 1998. Rusty Wallace sent Gordon into the wall as the No. 24 car was passing for the lead. Gordon was forced to park his severely damaged car and finished the race in 37th—his worst finish during the 1998 season.

Gordon at Sears Point Raceway

Though Sears Point Raceway is just a short drive from his birthplace in Vallejo, California, Jeff Gordon wasn't born for racing on Winston Cup road courses. It just seems that way.

With his breezy four-second victory at Sears Point during the 2000 season, Gordon extended his victory streak to a track-record three straight at Sears Point and an overall NASCAR-record six straight on road courses (a string broken two months later at Watkins Glen, where he finished 23rd). During his six-win span, Gordon won three poles and led 312 of 606 laps.

Though Gordon was developing into one of the strongest road-course racers on the Winston Cup circuit, an intense testing session at Sears Point in 1998 pushed him over the top. Since he and his Hendrick Motorsports crew landed in the Sonoma Valley three years ago for that testing session, only one other driver has visited Victory Lane at a road course.

Such dominance was not foretold for Gordon. A veteran of short-track open-wheel racing during his formative years, he was raised almost exclusively on ovals. His first two attempts at Sears Point yielded less-than-dominating finishes of 11th in 1993 and 37th after mechanical problems in 1994. Gordon soon figured out the road courses and is now considered the smoothest road course racer in the series.

Gordon's Sears Point Record Book— All-Time
(min. 5 starts)

Category	Total	Rank	All-Time Track Leader*
Money Won	$607,465	1st	(Mark Martin—584,130)
Starts	8	24th	11 tied with 12 Starts
Total Points	1,227	11th	Mark Martin—1,758
Avg. Start	5.3	1st	(Ricky Rudd—5.4)
Avg. Finish	7.8	1st	(Dale Earnhardt— 8.6)
Wins	3	1st	(E. Irvan, R. Wallace— 2)
Winning Pct.	37.5	1st	(B. Allison, E. Irvan—20.0)
Top 5s	5	4th	Martin, Rudd, R. Wallace—7
Top 10s	6	5th	Mark Martin—10
DNFs	1	17th	Hershel McGriff—4
Poles	2	2nd	Ricky Rudd—4
Front Row Starts	2	6th	Ricky Rudd—6
Laps Led	183	1st	(Mark Martin—160)
Pct. Led	25.9	1st	(Mark Martin—15.9)
Races Led	4	3rd	Rusty Wallace— 8
Times Led	9	3rd	Rusty Wallace—15
Times Led Most Laps	3	T-1st	(Rusty Wallace—3)
Bonus Points	35	2nd	Rusty Wallace—55
Laps Completed	691	21st	Michael Waltrip—996
Pct. of Laps Completed	97.9	13th	Johnny Benson—100.0
Points per Race	153.4	1st	(Mark Martin—146.5)
Lead Lap Finishes	7	10th	Dale Earnhardt—11

* Second-place driver or co-leader listed in parentheses if Gordon is track leader.

Memorable Sears Point Moment —1998 Save Mart/Kragen 350

Besides giving Gordon his first Sears Point win, the 1998 race offered some of the best road course racing in recent memory as Gordon and Bobby Hamilton battled in the final laps. After running down Hamilton, Gordon attempted to take the lead with 10 laps remaining. The two drivers bumped entering and exiting the hairpin Turn 11, with Gordon emerging with the lead. Hamilton clung to Gordon's rear bumper and again traded paint with the 24 car in Turn 11 on the next lap. On fresher tires, Gordon eventually pulled away for the win.

Gordon's Performance in Road Course Races Since 1993

Category	Gordon's Total	Gordon's Rank	Category Leader*
Avg. Start	5.6	1st	(Mark Martin—6.3)
Avg. Finish	8.4	2nd	Mark Martin—5.6
Poles	3	2nd	Mark Martin—4
Wins	6	1st	(Mark Martin—4)
Top 5s	10	2nd	Mark Martin—12
Top 10s	12	2nd	Mark Martin—15
Laps Led	329	2nd	(Mark Martin—347)

* Second-place driver or co-leader listed in parentheses if Gordon is the category leader

Gordon Track Performance Chart

Sears Point Raceway

Sonoma, California— 1.949 miles— Road Course

Year	Date	Race	St.	Fin.	Total Laps	Laps Completed	Laps Led	Condition	Money	Pts.	Bonus Pts.
1993	May 16	Save Mart Supermarkets 300K	15	11	74	74	0	Running	$10,215	130	0
1994	May 15	Save Mart 300	6	37	74	59	0	DNF—Rear End	12,675	52	0
1995	May 7	Save Mart 300	5	3	74	74	0	Running	41,625	165	0
1996	May 5	Save Mart 300	6	6	74	74	12	Running	48,145	155	5
1997	May 5	Save Mart Supermarkets 300	3	2	74	74	0	Running	66,065	170	0
1998	Jun 28	Save Mart/Kragen 300K	1	1	112	112	48	Running	160,675	185	10
1999	Jun 27	SaveMart Supermarkets 300	1	1	112	112	80	Running	125,040	185	10
2000	Jun 25	SaveMart/Kragen 300	5	1	112	112	43	Running	143,025	185	10

In just eight seasons, Jeff Gordon has made an indelible impression on the NASCAR world, especially on Winston Cup road courses. Only Mark Martin can claim equal right-turn prowess.

Gordon at Talladega Superspeedway

Until the 2000 season, Talladega Superspeedway was largely resistant to Jeff Gordon's charms. The longest, toughest, meanest racetrack in NASCAR, the 2.66-mile Alabama track seemed to allow only the incomparable Dale Earnhardt to romance and conquer it. True, Gordon won the 1996 DieHard 500, but only after the field had been severely thinned by a wreck that claimed Earnhardt (who suffered a broken sternum) and other top cars. That 1996 race was also shortened due to rain and darkness. All in all, not exactly a stellar victory.

Otherwise, Gordon's performance was rather unremarkable. In his first 14 starts, he finished outside of the Top 10 more often than he had inside it. Among those eight non-Top 10s finishes were four DNFs, caused by engine problems and crashes, that resulted in finishes of 31st or worse. Also hurting Gordon's chances was a lack of "friends." That is, a lack of drafting partners who can push a driver to the front. The hyper-successful Gordon seemed incapable of finding fellow drivers interested in helping him win more races.

Then came the 2000 season. Though he struggled elsewhere, Gordon seemed to come alive at Talladega. In the spring race, he won from the 36th starting position, setting the track record for lowest starting spot in an eventual win. Gordon followed that victory with a fourth-place finish in the fall race. Making his effort impressive was his ability to climb from the 43rd starting position to the lead by lap 13.

Memorable Talladega Moments—2000 Winston 500

Stuck in ninth place with less than 10 laps to go, Gordon picked his way through the draft and claimed his second victory at Talladega. By winning from the 36th starting position, Gordon bettered the record set by Earnhardt for lowest starting spot in a victory. Earnhardt won the 1999 Winston 500 after starting 27th. Gordon sealed his win on lap 184 by jumping from third to first (leapfrogging second-place Jeremy Mayfield) and taking the lead from Mark Martin on a startling move to the apron along the track's front stretch.

Gordon's Talladega Point Record Book —The Modern Era
(min. 5 starts)

Category	Total	Rank	Modern Era Track Leader
Money Won	$1,203,665	3rd	Dale Earnhardt—3,081,045
Starts	16	52nd	Dave Marcis—56
Total Points	2,036	41st	Darrell Waltrip—6,297.25
Avg. Start	13.6	17th	Bobby Isaac—5.2
Avg. Finish	15.2	7th	Dale Earnhardt—12.4
Wins	2	8th	Dale Earnhardt—10
Winning Pct.	12.5	4th	Dale Earnhardt—22.7
Top 5s	7	16th	Dale Earnhardt—23
Top 10s	8	26th	Dale Earnhardt—27
DNFs	4	68th	Darrell Waltrip—23
Poles	0	—	Bill Elliott—8
Front Row Starts	1	27th	Bill Elliott—13
Laps Led	364	10th	Dale Earnhardt—1,391
Pct. Led	12.3	4th	Dale Earnhardt—17.0
Races Led	13	18th	Dale Earnhardt—38
Times Led	46	14th	Dale Earnhardt—203
Times Led Most Laps	2	7th	Dale Earnhardt—12
Bonus Points	75	16th	Dale Earnhardt—250
Laps Completed	2,708	46th	Dave Marcis—8,993
Pct. of Laps Completed	91.8	12th	Robert Pressley—96.4
Points per Race	127.3	16th	Donnie Allison—142.5
Lead Lap Finishes	10	21st	Dale Earnhardt—27

Gordon Track Performance Chart

Talladega Superspeedway

Talladega, Alabama— 2.66 miles— 33° banking

Year	Date	Race	St.	Fin.	Total Laps	Laps Completed	Laps Led	Condition	Money	Pts.	Bonus Pts.
1993	May 2	Winston 500	30	11	188	188	0	Running	$15,795	130	0
	Jul 25	DieHard 500	8	31	188	148	7	DNF—Engine	11,250	75	5
1994	May 1	Winston 500	40	24	188	184	3	Running	15,525	96	5
	Jul 24	DieHard 500	15	31	188	149	0	DNF— Engine	19,660	70	0
1995	Apr 30	Winston 500	6	2	188	188	12	Running	165,315	175	5
	Jul 23	DieHard 500	3	8	188	188	97	Running	42,375	152	10
1996	Apr 28	Winston Select 500	11	33	188	141	18	DNF—Crash	34,325	69	5
	Jul 28	DieHard 500	2	1	129	129	37	Running	272,550	180	5
1997	May 10	Winston 500	11	5	188	188	13	Running	54,440	160	5
	Oct 12	DieHard 500	8	35	188	153	3	Running	38,915	63	5
1998	Apr 26	DieHard 500	6	5	188	188	3	Running	74,490	160	5
	Oct 11	Winston 500	6	2	188	188	49	Running	86,245	175	5
1999	Apr 25	DieHard 500	13	38	188	112	0	DNF—Handling	55,250	49	0
	Oct 17	Winston 500	14	12	188	188	71	Running	75,675	137	10
2000	Apr 16	DieHard 500	36	1	188	188	25	Running	159,755	180	5
	Oct 15	Winston 500	8	4	188	188	26	Running	82,100	165	5

Gordon drives a heavily bandaged Dupont Chevy during the 1999 DieHard 500 at Talladega Superspeedway. Caught in an early wreck, Gordon completed just 112 laps and finished the race in 38th.

Gordon makes a qualifying run at Talladega. Gordon has started outside of the Top 30 a mere four times in his career. Three of those poor qualifying efforts have come at Talladega, including his all-time low 40th in 1994.

Gordon at Texas Motor Speedway

Jeff Gordon has proven at Texas Motor Speedway that sometimes it's better to be lucky than good. Gordon, the Winston Cup series' most dominant driver over the last five seasons, has had no luck at the Texas track. Perhaps it is more accurate to say Gordon has had nothing but racin' luck at TMS.

How dire is Gordon's lot? He has been caught up in a crash in all four Texas races. His 32.3 average finish is a whopping 42nd among his Winston Cup peers. Among drivers with two or more Texas starts, only Ernie Irvan (38.7) and Hut Stricklin (36.5) have worse finishing records.

Forget wins, Top 5s, and Top 10s. Forget even Top 20s. For Gordon, recording a Top 25 proved to be an accomplishment, which he finally achieved in 2000 when he limped to a 25th-place finish. During this same span (1997 to 2000), Gordon had 33 wins on the other 20 Winston Cup tracks.

Gordon's bio at Texas is a litany of bad luck. In 1997, Gordon led 69 laps and looked solid until getting caught up in an Irvan crash. In 1998, with water seeping through the pavement, he was collected in that season's opening lap melee in Turn 1. In 1999, during a sustained march to the front, Gordon's right-front gave out and sent the No. 24 car crashing hard into the wall coming out of Turn 4. In 2000, a wreck on lap 111 ended his competitive hopes.

Gordon's Texas Record Book—All-Time
(min. 2 starts)

Category	Total	Rank	All-Time Track Leader
Money Won	$263,250	23rd	Jeff Burton—785,675
Starts	4	T-1st	25 others with 4 Starts
Total Points	270	28th	B. Labonte, T. Labonte—652
Avg. Start	12.5	9th	Steve Park—4.5
Avg. Finish	32.3	42nd	Bobby Labonte—4.3
Wins	0	—	J. Burton, T. Labonte, Martin, Earnhardt, Jr.—1
Winning Pct.	0.0	—	Earnhardt Jr.—100.0
Top 5s	0	—	Bobby Labonte—3
Top 10s	0	—	B. Labonte, T. Labonte—4
DNFs	2	2nd	Ernie Irvan—3
Poles	0	—	Irwin, Jarrett, Mayfield, T. Labonte—1
Front Row Starts	1	T-1st	7 others with 1 Front Row St.
Laps Led	69	7th	Terry Labonte—231
Pct. Led	5.2	7th	Terry Labonte—17.3
Races Led	1	13th	Dale Jarrett—4
Times Led	2	12th	Mark Martin—13
Times Led Most Laps	0	—	Terry Labonte—2
Bonus Points	5	14th	Terry Labonte—25
Laps Completed	887	25th	B. Labonte, T. Labonte—1,336
Pct. of Laps Completed	66.4	39th	B. Labonte, T. Labonte, Stewart—100.0
Points per Race	67.5	40th	B. Labonte, T. Labonte—163.0
Lead Lap Finishes	0	—	B. Labonte, T. Labonte—4

* Second-place driver or co-leader listed in parentheses if Gordon is track leader.

Memorable Texas Moment—1999 Primestar

Gordon finished a career-worst 43rd, and anti-Gordonism hit an all-time low when a cut right front tire sent Gordon into the outside wall coming off of turn 4 on lap 69. As Gordon's battered car skidded and spun through the grass along the front stretch, fans erupted into a gleeful ovation in reaction to the driver's misfortune. Groggy and in obvious pain, the 28-year-old driver was greeted by a derisive crowd as he gingerly removed himself from the car. He suffered bruised ribs and called the hit one of the hardest of his career.

"He's got so much natural ability; it kind of pisses me off."
—Ken Schrader, *Winston Cup Scene*

Gordon Track Performance Chart

Texas Motor Speedway

Fort Worth, Texas— 1.5 miles— 24° banking

Year	Date	Race	St.	Fin.	Total Laps	Laps Completed	Laps Led	Condition	Money	Pts.	Bonus Pts.
1997	Apr 6	Interstate Batteries 500	2	30	334	247	69	Running	$60,200	78	5
1998	Apr 5	Texas 500	17	31	334	252	0	DNF—Handling	66,900	70	0
1999	Mar 28	Primestar 500	8	43	334	68	0	DNF—Crash	60,000	34	0
2000	Apr 2	DirecTV 500	23	25	334	320	0	Running	76,150	88	0

Texas can safely be called Jeff Gordon's nightmare track. In the track's first four events, Gordon got caught in wrecks. His average finish in those four races was 32.2, his worst on any track.

Gordon at Watkins Glen International

The road course at Watkins Glen International brought a certain completeness to the young career of Jeff Gordon in 1997. Gordon's win in The Bud at The Glen that season by 1.3 seconds over New York-native Geoffrey Bodine marked the 26-year-old driver's first-ever victory on a NASCAR non-oval.

In his first four seasons, Gordon had won just about everywhere on every kind of track, from short tracks (such as Martinsville, Bristol, North Wilkesboro, and Richmond) to superspeedways (Daytona, Indianapolis, Pocono, and Talladega), from flat tracks (New Hampshire) to semi-banked speedways (California and Michigan) to high-banked monsters (Atlanta, Charlotte, Darlington, Dover, and Rockingham). His performance on tracks requiring right turns, however, took longer to develop.

A committed oval driver since his childhood, Gordon struggled but improved in his early road course races at Sears Point and Watkins Glen. At the Glen, he exited his first start after experiencing engine troubles (finishing 31st), but then finished the next six WGI races in the Top 10. By 1997, after consecutive Top 5 finishes, Gordon seemed poised to break out of his road-course shutout.

Indeed, Gordon has become the most dominant road courser on the Winston Cup circuit today. He won an unprecedented six straight road course races and tied Mark Martin's record of three straight Watkins Glen victories. In the modern era, only Rusty Wallace has as many road course wins as Gordon.

Memorable Watkins Glen Moment —2000 Global Crossing at The Glen

Going for an amazing seventh-straight road course wins, and a record four straight at Watkins Glen, Gordon saw his attempt at history cut short after being steered into the inside wall between turns 3 and 4 by Tony Stewart. Attempting a pass on the race's second lap, Gordon got side-by-side with Stewart through Watkins Glen's narrow ess turns. Stewart got loose, bumped Gordon while trying to correct, then appeared to continue deliberately bumping Gordon until Gordon's car smacked the guardrail. Gordon fell a lap down with a damaged car, but was able to get back on the lead lap and finish 23rd. Even more memorable than the on-track incident was the shouting match between the two Indiana drivers after the race.

Modern Era Road Course Wins

Driver	No. of Wins
Jeff Gordon	6
Rusty Wallace	6
Bobby Allison	5
Tim Richmond	5
Ricky Rudd	5
Darrell Waltrip	5

Gordon's Watkins Glen Record Book—All-Time
(min. 5 starts)

Category	Total	Rank	All-Time Track Leader*
Money Won	$571,860	2nd	Mark Martin—734,715
Starts	8	27th	6 tied with 15 Starts
Total Points	1,187	16th	Mark Martin—2,093
Avg. Start	5.9	1st	(Mark Martin—6.2)
Avg. Finish	9.1	2nd	Mark Martin—5.2
Wins	3	T-1st	(Mark Martin—3)
Winning Pct.	37.5	1st	(Mark Martin—23.1)
Top 5s	5	4th	Mark Martin—11
Top 10s	6	6th	Mark Martin—12
DNFs	1	30th	Derrike Cope—6
Poles	1	4th	D. Earnhardt, M. Martin—3
Front Row Starts	1	8th	Mark Martin—4
Laps Led	146	2nd	Mark Martin—204
Pct. Led	20.3	1st	(Mark Martin—18.0)
Races Led	4	7th	Rusty Wallace—9
Times Led	11	4th	M. Martin, R. Wallace—16
Times Led Most Laps	3	T-1st	(Mark Martin—3)
Bonus Points	35	5th	Rusty Wallace—55
Laps Completed	694	23rd	Dale Earnhardt—1,310
Pct. of Laps Completed	96.4	15th	Darrell Waltrip—100.0
Points per Race	148.4	2nd	Mark Martin—161.0
Lead Lap Finishes	7	13th	D. Earnhardt, D. Waltrip—14

* Second-place driver or co-leader listed in parentheses if Gordon is track leader.

Gordon Track Performance Chart

Watkins Glen International

Watkins Glen, New York— 2.454 miles— Road Course

Year	Date	Race	St.	Fin.	Total Laps	Laps Completed	Laps Led	Condition	Money	Pts.	Bonus Pts.
1993	Aug 8	The Budweiser at the Glen	11	31	90	64	0	DNF—Engine	$7,290	70	0
1994	Aug 14	The Bud at the Glen	3	9	90	90	0	Running	19,950	138	0
1995	Aug 13	The Bud at the Glen	5	3	90	90	4	Running	42,205	170	5
1996	Aug 11	The Bud at the Glen	5	4	90	90	0	Running	44,370	160	0
1997	Aug 10	The Bud at the Glen	11	1	90	90	32	Running	139,120	185	10
1998	Aug 9	The Bud at the Glen	1	1	90	90	55	Running	152,970	185	10
1999	Aug 15	Frontier at the Glen	3	1	90	90	55	Running	119,860	185	10
2000	Aug 13	Global Crossing @ The Glen	8	23	90	90	0	Running	46,095	94	0

Ricky Rudd, Rusty Wallace, and Mark Martin have been modern-era front runners on road courses. But Gordon's recent string of road course performances towers over all of his Winston Cup rivals, and it proves how well-rounded of a racer he is. Gordon posted three consecutive victories at Watkins Glen from 1997 to1999. *Nigel Kinrade*

Jeff Gordon's Performance in the Most Prestigious Winston Cup Events

On the Winston Cup schedule, there are races, and then there are events. In the NASCAR world, the biggest events are the season-opening Daytona 500, the Memorial day Coca-Cola 600 and the Labor Day Southern 500. While other races are popular or important to the Winston Cup Schedule- races such as the Brickyard 400, the Bristol night race and the Talledega races- none has yet reached the prestige of the Big Three.

This section details Gordon's career in the Major Races. listing career statistics, season-by-season totals and individual race performances. For each of Gordon's starts, the following details are listed: year, date, start, finish, total laps, laps completed, laps led, race-ending condition, series championship points and bonus points. For each season, total points, final standing and money earned are listed.

The high banks of Daytona never struck much fear in Jeff Gordon. He won his first start ever there, the 1993 Twin 125, and finished fifth in his first Daytona 500. He went on to win two 500s, in 1997 and 1999.

Gordon in the Daytona 500

One reason for Jeff Gordon's considerable reputation within NASCAR circles is his performance during Speed Weeks at Daytona each February. In his first Daytona race ever, the 1993 Twin 125s, he won. In his first Daytona 500, he led the first lap and finished in fifth. In 1999, Gordon became the first driver since Bill Elliott in 1987 to win the 500 from the pole. Also in 1999, he won the largest prize in American motor sports history: $2,172,246 (broken in 2000 by Dale Jarrett). Without question, Gordon has made an impact on the Great American Race in a very short time.

Of course, Daytona giveth and Daytona taketh away. The flip side of Gordon's success is a regular dose of reality. In eight Daytona 500s, his performance is symmetrically split: four Top 5s and four finishes of 16th or worse (including 42nd in 1996).

Ultimately, all other memories of Gordon at Daytona in February will be washed out by two moments: his Twin 125 win as a rookie and his incredible move on Rusty Wallace in the 1999 500. In a career filled with memorable moments, "The Move," in which Gordon dipped nearly to the tri-oval grass to make a pass on Wallace, is the most memorable.

Gordon's Daytona 500 Record Book—The Modern Era
(min. 5 starts)

Category	Total	Rank	Modern Era Event Leader*
Money Won	$3,200,717	2nd	Dale Earnhardt—3,470,455
Starts	8	47th	D. Marcis, D. Waltrip—28
Total Points	1,005	42nd	D. Earnhardt, D. Waltrip—3,106
Avg. Start	8.5	3rd	Davey Allison—7.7
Avg. Finish	15.6	9th	Jody Ridley—9.7
Wins	2	5th	Richard Petty—4
Winning Pct.	25.0	T-1st	(Dale Jarrett—25.0)
Top 5s	4	10th	Dale Earnhardt—12
Top 10s	4	23rd	Dale Earnhardt—16
DNFs	1	97th	A.J. Foyt—13
Poles	1	7th	B. Baker, B. Elliott, K. Schrader—3
Front Row Starts	1	16th	Do. Allison, D. Earnhardt, B. Elliott—4
Laps Led	183	9th	Dale Earnhardt—669
Pct. Led	11.4	5th	Buddy Baker
Races Led	6	14th	Dale Earnhardt—18
Times Led	13	20th	Dale Earnhardt—88
Times Led Most Laps	0	—	B. Allison, B. Baker, D. Earnhardt—3
Bonus Points	30	16th	Dale Earnhardt—105
Laps Completed	1,407	46th	Darrell Waltrip—4,726
Pct. of Laps Completed	87.9	20th	Ricky Craven—99.7
Points per Race	125.6	12th	Cale Yarborough—142.7
Lead Lap Finishes	5	13th	Dale Earnhardt—14

* Second-place driver or co-leader listed in parentheses if Gordon is track leader.

Gordon Daytona 500 Performance Chart

Daytona 500
Daytona International Speedway

Year	Date	St.	Fin.	Total Laps	Laps Completed	Laps Led	Condtition	Money	Pts.	Bonus Pts.
1993	Feb 14	3	5	200	200	2	Running	$111,150	160	5
1994	Feb 20	6	4	200	200	7	Running	112,525	165	5
1995	Feb 19	4	22	200	199	61	Running	67,915	102	5
1996	Feb 18	8	42	200	13	0	DNF—Handling	59,052	37	0
1997	Feb 16	6	1	200	200	40	Running	456,999	180	5
1998	Feb 15	29	16	200	200	56	Running	114,730	120	5
1999	Feb 14	1	1	200	200	17	Running	2,172,246	180	5
2000	Feb 20	11	34	200	195	0	Running	106,100	61	0

Gordon in the Coca-Cola 600

Jeff Gordon's performance in the Winston Cup series' major races has been remarkable since he joined the circuit in 1993. In his rookie season, he wasted no time in making a lasting first impression during his first Daytona 500 experience. Gordon's pattern was the same at Charlotte: make an immediate impact, then follow up that first impression with consistent excellence. In his first Coca-Cola 600, Gordon finished second (after starting 21st). In the next seven 600s, he nabbed five poles (consecutively) and won three times. His win in 1994 was the first of his Winston Cup career.

Performance in the Major Races (since 1993)
Gordon in the Coca-Cola 600, Daytona 500, and Southern 500

Category	Total	Rank	Category Leader*
Avg. Start	7.2	1st	(Dale Earnhardt—7.5)
Avg. Finish	11.0	2nd	Dale Earnhardt—9.2
Poles	6	1st	(Dale Jarrett—4)
Wins	9	1st	(Dale Jarrett—4)
Top 5s	14	1st	(D. Earnhardt, D. Jarrett—13)
Top 10s	16	2nd	(Dale Earnhardt—18)
Laps Led	796	2nd	Dale Earnhardt—1,027

* Second-place driver or co-leader listed in parentheses if Gordon is the category leader

Gordon Track Performance Chart

Coca-Cola 600
Charlotte Motor Speedway

Year	Date	St.	Fin.	Total Laps	Laps Completed	Laps Led	Condition	Money	Pts.	Bonus Pts.
1993	May 30	21	2	400	400	3	Running	$79,050	175	5
1994	May 29	1	1	400	400	16	Running	196,500	180	5
1995	May 28	1	33	400	283	37	DNF—Suspension	64,950	69	5
1996	May 26	1	4	400	400	101	Running	118,200	165	5
1997	May 25	1	1	333	333	44	Running	224,900	180	5
1998	May 24	1	1	400	400	53	Running	429,950	180	5
1999	May 30	10	39	400	341	1	DNF—Handling	56,780	51	5
2000	May 28	14	10	400	400	4	Running	78,950	139	5

> **"They're going to have to serve milk at the awards banquet instead of champagne."**
> —Dale Earnhardt, commenting on the youthfulness of 24-year-old champion Jeff Gordon, *Atlanta Journal and Constitution*

Gordon's Coca-Cola 600 Record Book—The Modern Era
(min. 5 starts)

Category	Total	Rank	Modern Era Event Leader*
Starts	8	46th	Darrell Waltrip— 28
Total Points	1,139	37th	Darrell Waltrip—3,751.25
Avg. Start	6.3	2nd	David Pearson—2.8
Avg. Finish	11.4	3rd	Bobby Labonte—10.5
Wins	3	2nd	Darrell Waltrip—5
Winning Pct.	37.5	1st	(Darrell Waltrip—17.9)
Top 5s	5	10th	Darrell Waltrip—11
Top 10s	6	16th	Darrell Waltrip—15
DNFs	2	67th	Dave Marcis—15
Poles	5	2nd	David Pearson—6
Front Row Starts	5	2nd	David Pearson—9
Laps Led	259	17th	Dale Earnhardt—975
Pct. Led	8.3	9th	Davey Allison—15.2
Races Led	8	11th	Dale Earnhardt—16
Times Led	25	11th	Dale Earnhardt—72
Times Led Most Laps	0	—	Bobby Allison—4
Bonus Points	40	13th	Dale Earnhardt—95
Laps Completed	2,957	40th	Darrell Waltrip—10,317
Pct. of Laps Completed	94.4	5th	Ernie Irvan—97.5
Points per Race	142.4	5th	David Pearson—146.9
Lead Lap Finishes	6	4th	Dale Earnhardt—10

* Second-place driver or co-leader listed in parentheses if Gordon is track leader.

Night racing in Charlotte has been a Jeff Gordon favorite. He finished second in his first 600, then won five consecutive poles and three races in his next seven 600 starts.

Gordon in the Southern 500

Jeff Gordon's success, in major races and not-so-major races, has been so widespread that it is difficult to declare one accomplishment as being automatically more impressive than the others. That indistinguishable ended after Gordon's win in the 1998 Southern 500. Run continuously since 1950, making it the oldest NASCAR event, the Southern 500 administers a unique historical test to Winston Cup competitors season after season. Achieving a first at the Southern 500 can distinguish a career. Gordon set the most impressive record in 500 history when he won the event four times in a row from 1995 to 1998. There have been five other repeat winners in event's history; none of them got past two straight wins.

Southern 500 Repeat Winners

Driver	Seasons
Jeff Gordon	1995–96–97–98
Bobby Allison	1971–72
Dale Earnhardt	1989–90
David Pearson	1976–77
Herb Thomas	1954–55
Cale Yarborough	1973–74

Gordon's Southern 500 Record Book—The Modern Era
(min. 5 starts)

Category	Total	Rank	Modern Era Event Leader*
Starts	8	48th	Darrell Waltrip— 47
Total Points	1,266	33rd	Bill Elliott—3,326
Avg. Start	6.9	2nd	David Pearson—4.7
Avg. Finish	6.1	1st	Jeff Burton—8.9
Wins	4	T-1st	(Cale Yarborough—4)
Winning Pct.	50.0	1st	(Cale Yarborough— 26.7)
Top 5s	5	10th	B. Elliott, D. Earnhardt—10
Top 10s	6	17th	Bill Elliott—16
DNFs	0	—	H.B. Bailey, B. Baker—9
Poles	0	—	David Pearson—5
Front Row Starts	1	14th	B. Elliott, D. Pearson—6
Laps Led	354	10th	Dale Earnhardt—1,138
Pct. Led	12.7	6th	Cale Yarborough—17.0
Races Led	7	15th	Bill Elliott—17
Times Led	20	11th	Darrell Waltrip—56
Times Led Most Laps	0	—	Dale Earnhardt—5
Bonus Points	35	16th	B. Elliott, D. Waltrip—95
Laps Completed	2,778	40th	Darrell Waltrip—8,252
Pct. of Laps Completed	99.8	1st	(Jeff Burton—99.0)
Points per Race	158.3	1st	(Bobby Allison—151.7)
Lead Lap Finishes	6	8th	Bill Elliott—12

* Second-place driver or co-leader listed in parentheses if Gordon is track leader.

Gordon Track Performance Chart

Southern 500
Darlington Raceway

Year	Date	St.	Fin.	Total Laps	Laps Completed	Laps Led	Condition	Money	Pts.	Bonus Pts.
1993	Sept 5	15	22	351	346	3	Running	$8,870	102	5
1994	Sept 4	7	6	367	366	0	Running	22,765	150	0
1995	Sept 3	5	1	367	367	54	Running	70,630	180	5
1996	Sept 1	2	1	367	367	52	Running	99,630	180	5
1997	Aug 31	7	1	367	367	116	Running	1,131,330	180	5
1998	Sept 6	5	1	367	367	64	Running	1,134,655	180	5
1999	Sept 5	4	13	270	270	41	Running	53,410	129	5
2000	Sept 3	10	4	328	328	24	Running	82,540	165	5

Gordon distinguished himself by winning four straight Southern 500s, an event run continuously since 1950. Of the five other repeat winners in the event's history, none has managed to win the race more than two times in a row.

"I'll be honest. I tried to knock the shit out of him when he hit me. I tried to put him in the wall, and I just missed him."
—Jeff Burton, on his famous last-lap tangle with Gordon during the 1998 Southern 500, *Winston Cup Scene*

117

Jeff Gordon's Performance in All-Star and Qualifying Events

Adding spice to the Winston Cup schedule is a collection of nonpoints races that, despite having no direct effect on the championship, are nevertheless run with an unbridled urgency sometimes missing from regular point-paying events. Two of the three nonpoints races currently on the schedule, the Bud Shootout and the Winston, are all-star races. The third, the Twin 125 qualifying race, determines the driver's starting spot in the series' most important event, the Daytona 500.

This section details Gordon's career performance in these races. For each event, Gordon's effort is broken down via a performance chart and summarized in 12 statistical categories. The performance chart lists the year, date, race name, along with Gordon's start, finish, total laps, laps completed, laps led, race-ending condition, and money earned.

Deviating from the No. 24 car's familiar rainbow look, Gordon sported a special paint scheme for the 1997 Busch Clash at Daytona. Held a week before the season-opening Daytona 500, the Busch Clash (now called the Bud Shootout) is a yearly exhibition race that pits the previous season's pole winners in a sprint race. In 1997, with the new paint scheme, Gordon led the final nine laps en route to his second career Clash win.

Gordon Race Performance Chart

Busch Clash & Bud Shootout

Daytona International Speedway

Year	Date	Race	St.	Fin.	Total Laps	Laps Completed	Laps Led	Condition	Money
1994	Feb 13	Busch Clash	6	1	20	20	2	Running	$54,000
1995	Feb 12	Busch Clash	5	4	20	20	1	Running	42,000
1996	Feb 11	Busch Clash	17	9	20	20	0	Running	15,500
1997	Feb 9	Busch Clash	13	1	20	20	9	Running	54,000
1998	Feb 8	Bud Shootout	5	14	25	24	15	DNF—Engine	19,500
1999	Feb 7	Bud Shootout	8	15	25	10	2	DNF—Quit	22,000
2000	Feb 13	Bud Shootout	6	2	25	25	9	Running	57,500

Gordon in the Bud Shootout

Races Run	7
Victories	2
Winning Pct.	28.6
Total Winnings	$264,500
Top 5s	4
Top 10s	5
DNFs	2
Average Start	8.6
Average Finish	6.6
Races Led	6
Laps Led (Pct.)	38 (24.5)
Laps Completed (Pct.)	139 (89.7)

"I don't know what people are expecting out of him, if he's going to be greater than sliced bread, or what. I don't think he's going to be no better driver than Richard Petty was. He's a good driver. But he'd have to win 200-plus races and seven or eight championships to overcome that. He's got a long way to go. Winning one championship doesn't make him the greatest driver in the world."

—Dale Earnhardt, *Arizona Republic*

Jeff Gordon celebrates his second career Busch Clash win in 1997. The Busch Clash (now the Bud Shootout) is another event in which Gordon has excelled. He has driven to 5 top 10s in seven starts. *Nigel Kinrade*

Gordon in the Twin 125s

Races Run	8
Victories	1
Winning Pct.	12.5
Total Winnings	$165,893
Poles	1
Top 5s	6
Top 10s	7
DNFs	0
Average Start	7.4
Average Finish	4.4
Races Led	3
Laps Led (Pct.)	80 (20)
Laps Completed (Pct.)	400 (100)

Gordon shocked the Winston Cup world in 1993 by winning the first Twin 125 qualifying race of his career. He started sixth and led the final 29 laps. While Gordon hasn't won a 125 since, his consistency has been remarkable. His average finish is 4.4 in Daytona qualifying races.

Gordon Race Performance Chart

Twin 125s

Daytona International Speedway

Year	Date	Race	St.	Fin.	Total Laps	Laps Completed	Laps Led	Condition	Money
1993	Feb 18	Twin 125—No. 1	6	1	50	50	29	Running	$35,200
1994	Feb 17	Twin 125—No. 2	13	3	50	50	0	Running	15,200
1995	Feb 16	Twin 125—No. 2	7	2	50	50	0	Running	20,000
1996	Feb 15	Twin 125—No. 2	3	4	50	50	0	Running	11,122
1997	Feb 13	Twin 125—No. 2	11	2	50	50	0	Running	25,589
1998	Feb 12	Twin 125—No. 1	6	15	50	50	12	Running	10,330
1999	Feb 11	Twin 125—No. 1	1	2	50	50	39	Running	30,931
2000	Feb 17	Twin 125—No. 1	12	6	50	50	0	Running	17,521

Gordon Race Performance Chart

The Winston
Charlotte Motor Speedway

Year	Date	Race	St.	Fin.	Total Laps	Laps Completed	Laps Led	Condition	Money
1994	May 21	The Winston Open	6	1	50	50	21	Running	$28,000
		The Winston	15	14	70	70	0	Running	18,000
1995	May 20	The Winston	7	1	70	70	49	Running	300,000
1996	May 18	The Winston	5	8	70	70	0	Running	21,500
1997	May 17	The Winston	19	1	70	70	9	Running	207,500
1998	May 16	The Winston	4	12	70	70	36	Running	83,500
1999	May 22	The Winston	2	3	70	70	34	Running	160,000
2000	May 20	The Winston	11	16	70	62	0	DNF—Crash	30,110

Gordon in the Winston*

Races Run	7
Victories	2
Winning Pct.	28.6
Total Winnings	$820,610
Poles	0
Top 5s	3
Top 10s	4
DNFs	1
Average Start	9
Average Finish	7.9
Races Led	4
Laps Led (Pct.)	128 (26.1)
Laps Completed (Pct.)	482 (98.4)

* — Excludes the Winston Open

"There's no denying how talented he is. ... Anyone who would run Jeff down as far as his driving or talents or potential future in this sport is just plain jealous because he's a potential superstar."
—Ken Schrader, Winston Cup driver and former Gordon teammate, *Arizona Republic*

IROC

Chapter 7

Jeff Gordon's Performance in the International Race of Champions Series

Adding spice to the Winston Cup schedule is a collection of nonpoints races that, despite having no direct effect on the championship, are nevertheless run with an unbridled urgency sometimes missing from regular point-paying events. Two of the three nonpoints races currently on the schedule, the Bud Shootout and the Winston, are all-star races. The third, the Twin 125 qualifying race, determines the driver's starting spot in the series' most important event, the Daytona 500.

This section details Gordon's career performance in these races. For each event, Gordon's effort is broken down via a performance chart and summarized in 12 statistical categories. The performance chart lists the year, date, race name, along with Gordon's start, finish, total laps, laps completed, laps led, race-ending condition, and money earned.

Gordon, in the No. 10 dark blue car, tries to secure the second position behind Eddie Cheever (No. 11 Aqua) during intense IROC 2000 action at Talladega. Battling with Gordon are Greg Ray (No. 9 Orange), Mark Dismore (No. 12 Yellow), Dale Jarrett (No. 8 White), Bobby Labonte (No. 7 Violet), Dale Earnhardt Jr. (No. 5 Lime), Rusty Wallace (No. 6 Medium Blue), and Jeff Burton (No. 3 Dark Green).

Gordon's IROC Career

Victories	1
Winning Pct.	4.2
Races Run	24
Total Winnings	$275,000
Top 5s	12
DNFs	3
Average Finish	5.96
Races Led	12
Laps Led (Pct.)	52 (4.7)
Laps Completed (Pct.)	1,041 (94.98)
Total Points	257
Points per Race	10.7
Total Bonus Points	17

"Everybody's been looking for the next Richard Petty. Now they're looking for the next Jeff Gordon."
—Darrell Waltrip, *Fortune Magazine*

Career IROC Results

Year	Date	Track	St.	Fin.	Total Laps	Laps Completed	Laps Led	Condition	Pts.	Bonus Pts.
1995	Feb 17	Daytona International Speedway	12	11	40	28	4	DNF—Transmission	4	0
	Mar 25	Darlington Raceway	2	2	60	60	3	Running	20	3
	Apr 29	Talladega Superspeedway	7	5	38	38	10	Running	13	3
	Jul 29	Michigan Speedway	7	3	50	50	5	Running	14	0
Total Points: 51		**Final Standing:4th**				**Total Winnings: $50,000**				
1996	Feb 16	Daytona International Speedway	12	6	40	40	0	Running	9	0
	Apr 27	Talladega Superspeedway	7	7	38	6	2	DNF—Crash	8	0
	May 17	Charlotte Motor Speedway	5	5	67	67	0	Running	10	0
	Aug 17	Michigan Speedway	3	12	50	39	0	DNF— Mechanical	3	0
Total Points: 30		**Final Standing: 10th**				**Total Winnings: $40,000**				
1997	Feb 14	Daytona International Speedway	3	9	40	40	9	Running	9	3
	May 16	Charlotte Motor Speedway	4	3	67	67	0	Running	14	0
	Jun 21	California Speedway	9	5	50	50	0	Running	10	0
	Jul 27	Michigan Speedway	8	9	50	50	0	Running	6	0
Total Points: 39		**Final Standing: 6th**				**Total Winnings: $40,000**				
1998	Feb 13	Daytona International Speedway	6	1	30	30	2	Running	21	0
	May 2	California Speedway	12	3	50	50	5	Running	17	3
	Jun 13	Michigan Speedway	11	8	50	50	0	Running	7	0
	Jul 31	Indianapolis Motor Speedway	9	9	40	40	0	Running	6	0
Total Points: 51		**Final Standing: 3rd**				**Total Winnings: $60,000**				
1999	Feb 12	Daytona International Speedway	11	6	40	40	8	Running	12	3
	Apr 24	Talladega Superspeedway	7	4	38	38	1	Running	12	0
	Jun 11	Michigan Speedway	8	7	50	50	0	Running	8	0
	Aug 6	Indianapolis Motor Speedway	7	2	40	40	0	Running	17	0
Total Points: 49		**Final Standing: 5th**				**Total Winnings: $60,000**				
2000	Feb 18	Daytona International Speedway	6	10	40	40	0	Running	5	0
	Apr 15	Talladega Superspeedway	3	5	38	38	1	Running	10	0
	Jun 10	Michigan Speedway	6	7	50	50	0	Running	8	0
	Jul 27	Indianapolis Motor Speedway	5	4	40	40	2	Running	14	2
Total Points: 37		**Final Standing: 6th**				**Total Winnings: $40,00**				

Gordon walks to his assigned car before the second event of IROC 2000 at Talladega (he finished fifth). One of the few accomplishments to elude Gordon's grasp has been the IROC championship. In fact, he has struggled to find a comfort level in the series. In 24 races, Gordon had one win, at Daytona in 1998. That win was less than satisfying: Jeff Burton passed him on lap 31 when rain began to fall. Because rain eventually forced the race to be called, the finishing order was set based on the last completed lap, which was lap 30, when Gordon was in the lead.

Gordon and his wife, Brooke, walk down pit road to Gordon's assigned car before the second IROC 2000 race of the season at Talladega. Gordon finished the race in fifth and placed sixth in the final IROC 2000 point standings.

"He probably has as much or more raw talent as I've ever seen, and he doesn't have any bad habits. He's got the looks and the charm. But, mostly, he's got the ability."
—Rick Hendrick, Gordon's car owner, *Arizona Republic*

Sources and References

Armijo, Mark. "He's Young, Talented and Leading the Pack." *Arizona Republic*, October 29, 1995.

Assael, Shaun. "Pass or Fail." *ESPN Magazine*, March 8, 1999.

Bourcier, Bones. "Getting Personal with Jeff Gordon." *Stock Car Racing*, April 1995.

Cawthon, Raad. "Jeff Gordon, the Wonder Boy, is Riding a Pinnacle." *Philadelphia Inquirer*, February 14, 1998.

——. "Gordon Driving the Fast Track." *Atlanta Journal and Constitution*, February 28, 1993.

Charlotte Observer. 1989–1993. Race results.

Cohn, Bob. "New Kid on Engine Block Doesn't Faze Earnhardt." *Arizona Republic*, October 29, 1995.

Cotter, Tom. "Gordon Golden Again." *Road & Track*, February 1999.

Country.com. 1972–1999. http://www.country.com/motor/race/raceprior-f.html. Race results.

"Dominators of 1998." *Sport Magazine*, January 1999.

Fielden, Greg. *Forty Years of Stock Car Racing: Big Bucks and Boycotts, 1965–1971*. Vol. 3. Surfside Beach, S.C.: The Galfield Press, 1989.

——. *Forty Years of Stock Car Racing: Forty Plus Four, 1990–1993*. Surfside Beach, S.C.: The Galfield Press, 1994.

——. *Forty Years of Stock Car Racing: The Modern Era, 1972–1989*. Vol. 4. Surfside Beach, S.C.: The Galfield Press, 1990.

Fielden, Greg, and Peter Golenbock. *The Stock Car Racing Encyclopedia*. New York: MacMillan, Inc., 1997.

Hinton, Ed. "Nasty Traffic." *Sports Illustrated*, February 22, 1999.

Hummer, Steve. "Gordon's Coronation Gives Earnhardt Generation Gap to Close." *Atlanta Journal and Constitution*, November 13, 1995.

Ingram, Jonathan. "Ford Upset Gordon Defecting to Chevy." *Atlanta Journal and Constitution*, May 17, 1992.

Johnson, Roy S. "Speed Sells." *Fortune Magazine*, April 12, 1999.

Lopez, Steve. "Babes, Bordeaux and Billy Bobs." *Time*, May 31, 1999.

Mizell, Hubert. "'Jeff Who?' Is a Racing Wunderkind." *St. Petersburg Times*, February 12, 1993.

Thatsracin.com. 1996–2000. http://thatsracin.com. Race results archive.

"Turn Four." *Winston Cup Scene*, September 10, 1998.

Tuschak, Beth. "Gordon Gets Closer to First NASCAR Title." *USA Today*, November 10, 1995.

Whicker, Mark. "Asphalt Jungle Motor Sports." *Orange County Register*, August 9, 1998.

"Winston Cup 1997: Year in Review." *Winston Cup Scene*, December 4, 1997.

Winston Cup Scene. 1992–2000. Vol. 16, No. 1; Vol. 24, No. 30. Race results.

"Year in Review: 1995." *Winston Cup Scene*, December 14, 1995.

Author's Note on Sources and References

To achieve the level of statistical analysis that this book attempts, finding reliable sources of fundamental race data is essential. The core statistics of a race event—each driver's start, finish, money, laps completed, and laps led—must be secured for all races to create an extended, comprehensive look at a driver's career and his standing in stock car racing history. Taken together, the resources on the list above provided that core of statistics. In particular, Greg Fielden's monumental series *Forty Years of Stock Car Racing* is the seminal historical research achievement in the world of stock car racing. His work is the foundation for all works that have and will follow, including this book. Any author exploring stock car racing from a historical point of view is automatically indebted to Fielden's incomparable work.

Index

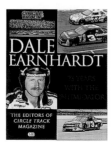

**Dale Earnhardt:
23 Years with
the Intimidator**
ISBN: 0-7603-1186-2

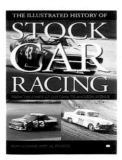

**Illustrated History of
Stock Car Racing**
ISBN: 0-7603-0416-5

Charlotte Motor Speedway
ISBN: 0-7603-0751-2

American Stock Car
ISBN: 0-7603-0977-9

Behind the Scenes of NASCAR
ISBN: 0-7603-0348-7

NASCAR Transporters
ISBN: 0-7603-0816-0

**Dale Earnhardt:
The Final Record**
ISBN: 0-7603-0953-1